DEANING

VAN CLEVE MORRIS

*Deaning*

MIDDLE MANAGEMENT IN ACADEME

UNIVERSITY OF ILLINOIS PRESS

URBANA, CHICAGO, LONDON

© 1981 BY THE BOARD OF TRUSTEES OF THE UNIVERSITY OF ILLINOIS

MANUFACTURED IN THE UNITED STATES OF AMERICA


LIBRARY OF CONGRESS CATALOGING IN PUBLICATION DATA

    Morris, Van Cleve.
       Deaning, middle management in academe.

       Includes index.
       1. Deans (in schools)—United States.
    I. Title.
    LB2341.M638    378'.112    80-26119
    ISBN 0-252-00871-5

TO CATH

# Contents

*Preface*

UNIVERSITIES in the United States are now big business. Over the years, they have drifted away from that precious ambiance of bucolic, ivied serenity and gradually assimilated their work to the tumble and texture of bureaucracy, American style.

With this development in higher education, as with other organizations, managerial skill has taken on a new, more urgent visibility. The modern university now needs a cadre of administrators to run it quite as much as it needs an army of scholars to think and teach. The knowledge industry has spread throughout the American socioeconomy, but the university is its headquarters. Basic decisions on the search for and dissemination of knowledge are the responsibility of headquarters personnel. Chief among these individuals are those who govern and administer our institutions of higher learning.

Somewhere in the inner zones of this cadre of administrators sits the academic dean. This individual is the critical fulcrum for protecting the mental health of a faculty and student body on the one hand and advancing the integrity and vitality of the larger organization on the other. The person who sits in this middle-management chair sees the swirl and exhilaration of university life perhaps more clearly than any other citizen of academia.

This book is about that person. In preparing this account, I have come to learn that writing about a dean's work is best accomplished if approached rather indirectly, like writing a memorandum to a friend. Accordingly, what follows is not intended to be a technical treatise on educational administration or a catalog of guidelines and how-to's on management duties. Rather, it might be described as a third-person account of a first-person experience, an individual perspective on an unlit corner of academic life written from inside the compound.

The initial draft was composed during an administrative sabbatical provided by the University of Illinois at Chicago Circle following my seven years as dean of the College of Education on that campus. I am indebted to B. J. Chandler, former dean of the School of Education at Northwestern University, for my appointment to the position of visiting scholar at his institution during this period and for the perquisites attaching to this honorary appointment, namely, a private office and the run of the Northwestern Library. I also wish to acknowledge the watchful assistance of Claude Mathis, director of the Center for the Teaching Professions at Northwestern. He kindly allowed me to try out some of this material on one of his doctoral seminars in higher-education faculty development. Finally, may I mention Emanuel Hurwitz, assistant dean *extraordinaire*, friend, counselor, and "all-'round savvy pro" in matters administrative, who shared in most of what is recounted here.

Many individuals—friends, colleagues, relatives—have participated in the review of this manuscript. Their critical suggestions—offered in good spirit and, may I say, abundance?—have been extremely helpful in designing this narrative.

Van Cleve Morris
Chicago, Illinois
December 8, 1980

DEANING

# ONE

# The Study of Academic Management

ADMINISTRATION is one of the new behavioral sciences. As things stand, we are not sure whether it is applied sociology, practicing social psychology, or, perhaps, a special variant of information engineering. Its placement in the epistemology of disciplines is still an open question.

Its origins as a subject matter are unclear. A generation ago, James Burnham, in *The Managerial Revolution*, developed the argument that a new social class was in the process of being born in the Western world. Communism and Capitalism, he said, were still arguing an essentially irrelevant question: Who should control the means of production, the masses or the propertied classes? And while the argument was going on, a new class of individuals—the managers— were quietly taking over. The word *control* was acquiring a new meaning, i.e., not the cornering of capital resources but rather the supervision of the process of production. It was not the capitalist who any longer called the shots but rather the manager he had hired to run the shop!

By now, of course, this is old stuff in the industrial sector. Corporations are governed by their managers, not by their stockholders. But the revolution that has overtaken business and industry has rolled on into the military, the government, and, of course, the educational establishment. In a predominantly service-oriented society, the expansion of managerial and administrative arrangements is by now commonplace. Indeed, administration is itself one of the marketable services in such an economy. In any event, the new *control class* is that group of individuals who have their hands on the levers of management within the organizations and institutions they inhabit. It is the behavior of these individuals that constitutes the new science.

This book examines administrative behavior in higher education. As we will see, the administration of a large, complex university bears only indirect resemblance to the administration of a bank, an army regiment, a government bureau, a trade union, or a manufacturing concern. Except for those constants which prevail throughout all organizational life— budgeting, payroll, plant and equipment maintenance—a university's managerial business is generated out of conditions not fully shared by other kinds of organizations.

For one thing, the service that a university is prepared to deliver is not intended for everybody. Unlike a hospital, an insurance company, or a can-opener factory, a university's service product is not for sale to every comer; you have to qualify to become a customer. In spite of our great Jacksonian advances over the last seventy-five years in the field of education, it is still true that a university education is genuinely usable by and therefore actually marketable to only one-third or, at the outside, one-half of the population. In our public documents, we pursue the dream that this half is distributed evenly through all socio-economic classes in the United States. It is true that scholarships, loans, and basic educational opportunity grants to low-income students exert an equalizing effect; but when the survivors are counted, it turns out that higher education's half continues to be the socio-economic *upper* half of the nation's young people. Unless a massive redistribution of both wealth and educational attainment is somehow ushered in, this selective tendency will

4

continue to operate. This means that, by the very nature of its service product, a university is upper-half oriented. Although it is middle-class in constitution and makeup, the university leans toward brains, organization, money, and power; and academic people want to keep it that way. Indeed, in a university, a large segment of the administrative workforce (the admissions apparatus) is assigned the specific task of maintaining this tilt. It performs this function by exercising tight control over the selection of new customers.

For another thing, the service a university delivers to its clientele is virtually unmeasurable. No one, least of all university professors and administrators, knows for sure when the service is actually being delivered and when it is not. The yield of a university's classrooms and research laboratories is a phantom element that resists being added up to a bottom line.[1] This means that the administrative arrangements of a university necessarily face inward toward *process* rather than outward toward *product*. The *input* of the faculty—degrees, government grants, teaching load, number of student advisees—and the *inner workings* of the organization—staff conferences, program reviews, seminars, committee meetings—become the primary counters. The *output*—that is, the competence of the graduate which is directly traceable to faculty effort—is a commodity on which all members of the organization are virtually silent. At least allusions to it are rarely seen in faculty promotion dossiers or proposals for outside funding. The only output susceptible to quantitative and qualitative measures is published research, but even the overall effect of this product on the wider community beyond the refereed journals is virtually unknowable. All of this adds up to the fact that administrative behavior in universities, unlike that in other organizations, must operate in

[1] Some years ago a student brought suit against Columbia University for failing to teach him wisdom, a promise which, he claimed, the university had extended in its elaborate catalog rhetoric. After some contentious litigation the student lost; but he apparently had made his point, since the university toned down some of its more gratuitous claims for a university education.

5

ignorance of the social impact and therefore the economic value,[2] if any, of whatever it is this behavior is administering.

For a third difference that is perhaps more directly germane to its managerial idiosyncrasies, a university's employees—those expected to deliver the service—are among the most intelligent and highly educated persons in the population; certainly they are among the top 5 percent. As a group they are highly verbal and inquisitive, resplendent of ego and hubris, and blessed with a well developed sense of both their own social importance and special rights as intellectuals in an essentially philistine social order. Moreover, since they are extremely touchy about their prerogatives, university professors typically take an active, day-to-day interest in the organizational structures that surround them. They know more about the organization for which they work and hold significantly stronger, more articulate views as to how it should operate than is true of their equivalent numbers in, say, the United States Navy, Sears Roebuck, the Ford Motor Company, or the Salvation Army.

Finally, and directly related to the preceding, a university's employees are much closer to the levers of power than is true of their counterparts in other organizations. There is a long history of faculty hegemony in academic institutions, reaching back to the medieval universities in Western Europe, and even today the governance of most of our institutions of higher learning is an uneasy partnership between the institutional structure of line-and-staff administrators on the one hand and the academic faculty strucure of departments, committees, councils, and senates on the other. In theory the latter apparatus is *advisory* to the former, but in practice the two hierarchies are jealous contestants for the upper hand. This feature of university life necessarily complicates institutional decisionmaking and renders much of organization

---

[2] In recent years, there has been a sharp erosion in the assumption that a university education is a good thing. See Caroline Bird, *The Case against College*, ed. Helene Mandelbaum (New York: D. McKay Co., 1975).

6

theory neither true nor false but merely irrelevant when applied to academic establishments.

As the above observations indicate, academic administration must be examined in the context of its peculiar conditions; and what is said about it, either in this book or elsewhere, possibly may not generalize to other circumstances. Moreover, this book focuses on academic administration from *inside the hierarchy*. Its target, as the subtitle suggests, is the managerial element that governs conduct within the pack. Most of the literature on academic administration pertains to managerial phenomena at the top executive level. Presidents and chancellors tend to be preoccupied with the more glamorous, business-oriented, public side of administration. They concern themselves with operating budgets, new buildings, higher tuition fees. Their responsibilities require the stroking of alumni, the appeasing of trustees, and the exhorting of football fans. In pursuit of their ends, they spend much of their time *outside* their institutions in the cultivation of mayors, legislators, governors, corporate executives, and government bureau chiefs. Deans, on the other hand, customarily spend most of their time *inside* their institutions. A dean functions in a pocket somewhere down in the bowels or, at the least, the thorax of the table of organization. Here is what the president brags about to newspaper reporters gets done.

The dean level of academic administration provides a unique vantage point from which to view the entire organization. For one thing, it is the only line position that enjoys *routine*, in contrast with *ad hoc*, contact with the full spectrum of organizational elements—students, faculty, department heads, fellow deans, vice-presidents, and president, not to mention staff persons at all levels. Also, a line dean still holds a faculty position, whereas administrators at higher levels, who usually make a final commitment to career administration, leave the teaching and research ranks for good and consider themselves fulltime managers. Finally, the deanship

7

is the seat of personnel administration, the heart of any organization. More than any other officer lower or higher in the hierarchy, a dean is the person responsible for the caliber of academic employees. Moreover, in daily work a dean deals primarily with people, not with paper. He or she is the highest officer in the hierarchy expected to have regular, operational contact with the faculty, the deliverers of the university's service. This close, everyday association with the central element of the institution's personnel puts the dean at the center of a university's raison d'etre, i.e., teaching and research. No higher officer enjoys this intimate proximity to the primary action of an academic institution.

Beyond these unique features of deaning, middle management in academe makes special intellectual and emotional demands on its participants. In Trumanesque terms, middle management in a university—among all administrative categories, lower and higher—represents a particular form of "heat in the kitchen." This book provides a look at the kitchen, with commentary on the source and nature of the heat, when cooling measures fail.

The problems flowing through a dean's office have a character all their own. A dean is that special breed of academic whose temperament and intellectual perspective are thought to be conducive to the proper management of these problems. But deaning is not necessarily an *ad hominem* business dependent for its success on merely personal style. It is also a work-a-day activity defined by institutional expectations that can be codified and discussed in a more or less orderly way. This book is designed to explore these expectations. In this sense it is a kind of "combat" manual for deans, a handbook on how to lose innocence gradually in the exciting and sometimes turbulent world of university deaning.

Chapter 2 explores the administrative temperament. Succeeding chapters examine different components of deanly work from the viewpoint of the middle manager.

By way of a procedural note, it is important for the reader to remember that the account to follow is drawn from ad-

ministrative experience in a large university, an institution
with several colleges all governed by one president and a
squad of vice-presidents. A generic organization chart for
such a campus looks like this:

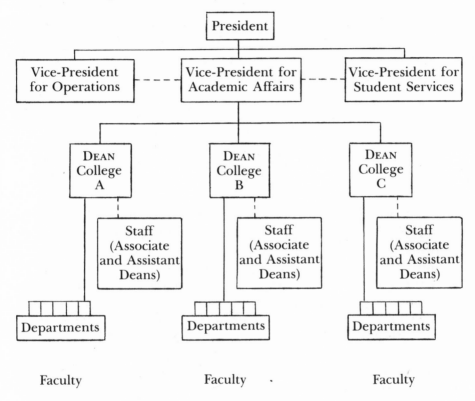

The allusions and references in the following pages are oriented to this arrangement. However, with a few adjustments
of titles and linkages, they can be interpreted so as to apply
to smaller, more deliberately single-purpose, institutions.

TWO

## The Administrative Temperament

ADMINISTRATORS are 51 percent born and 49 percent made. Like concert pianists or life-insurance salesmen, they bring some blend of basic traits to their work; but these traits must be cultivated, sharpened, and tested in performance before we say the individual is ready for service.

The preeminent ingredient all administrators bring to their jobs is ego. It requires a healthy self-concept to believe that one can lead a large group of people in any undertaking, most especially an academic enterprise in which rugged intellectual individualism and going one's own way are not only taken for granted, but are vigorously practiced every day, almost as a badge of honor. Unlike a corporation president or a symphony orchestra conductor, a university administrator does not work in a situation of organizational discipline. It is a looser context where personal idiosyncrasy and individual behavior are not readily susceptible to direction or control. Under these circumstances, leadership must rely on more subtle ingredients of personality—persuasion, empathy, listening ability, and emotional steadiness. But all of these must find their base in a strong, well-established sense of self in whoever sits in the administrator's chair.

It is ego, in fact, that accounts for the primary attractions of the job. Administrative work is executive in character, and it is therefore prestigious on its own account. It also pays a little more. But most important, it expands the realm of responsibility and therefore intensifies the total impact of one's person on the environment. In short, it provides status, a commodity concerning which no person is indifferent.

Faculty members are fond of scoffing at the administrator, ridiculing his or her endless committee meetings and allegedly trivial paper shuffling. Even deans will join in this self-deprecating form of ragging. But one will notice that there are very few voluntary resignations from deanships. And whenever a faculty member is mentioned as a potential candidate for such an opening, the scorn, at least from that individual, quickly melts into a self-conscious, touching availability. In academic life a middle-management position embraces precious little power, but it embraces some, and there isn't a faculty member alive who wouldn't be flattered at the thought of being eligible and ready for it.

The administrative ego is occasionally fortified by other somewhat extraneous considerations. Sometimes an individual will express a desire to be of service to the institution or will claim that the particular subject matter discipline out of which he or she comes is especially appropriate as a training ground for administrative work. The question is both flattering and intriguing: Is there something that psychology—or physics, history, or accounting—can tell us about being a dean? The answer is probably no, since escapees from all disciplines have become successful and unsuccessful deans.

The drive that propels people toward deaning and other administrative work is psychologically simple. It is a desire for visibility among one's fellow citizens. We usually call it ambition.

Ambition, however, is a tricky substance. In some individuals, it leaks out as mere conceit and hubris, probably going nowhere. In others, it is harnessed, organized, and systematically put to work by the individual for his or her own development. But ambition has a social vector also. As in politicians, it must be exhibited in socially acceptable ways. An individual cannot be too eager to dean, lest this very eagerness display signs that he or she may want the job for the wrong—purely personal—reasons. As with so many leadership positions, the aspirant must edge toward it as though it were being thrust upon an almost but not quite unwilling party.

Several career routes lead to deaning. The first and conventional pathway is the *professorial ascension* method. The assistant professor rises through academic ranks to become a full professor and department head; then, with scholarship and teaching achievements well established, he or she advances to the fulltime administrative post of deaning. The second, less frequently seen pathway, is that of the *trained administrator*, wherein the individual specializes in administration and management at the graduate level, develops a scholarly record in the study of administrative problems, and makes administration itself a career, starting with staff positions as assistant or associate dean before moving on to the dean level. For these individuals, the passage from "staff" to "line" responsibility is a severe, sometimes jolting transition. A third and even more rarely seen pathway is the *managerial outsider transfer*, in which a business executive, military officer, or school superintendent is called to a university to fill a dean's chair. These individuals face special problems, since they have learned to maintain a distance from their subordinates that is not typical of, nor indeed permitted in, the academic environment. A fourth and final pathway is via the purely *political appointment* of those who have made the right friends in the right places early in their careers. They fail as scholars and move on to become living paradigms of the Peter Principle,[1] much to the agony of all those around them.

Whatever the route of access, the arrival at a deanship sig-

---

[1] "In a hierarchy, every employee tends to rise to his level of incompetence." See Laurence J. Peter and Raymond Hill, *The Peter Principle* (New York: William Morrow & Co., 1969).

nals the onset of a major change in a person's life. Deaning, like other leadership posts, makes unusual demands. It is an exposed position that reveals the strengths and weaknesses of character as no job of lesser responsibility will do. Within this context of pressure we find the administrative temperament.

*   *   *

What qualities of mind and character are forced into play in the administrative setting? Although few in number, these qualities deserve extended commentary. Understandably, some of these qualities may be valuable at the professorial level as well, but typically they are not especially noted, and therefore not rewarded, there. They come to full prominence in the act of deaning.

One might be tagged the *general officer* syndrome. Although the analogy ought not be pressed too far, it is nevertheless instructive. We all know that the Army embraces a series of ranks, the top five of which are called general. In a military context the term *general* is to be taken literally—that is, at this level, the officer is lifted out of his specialty and is given general charge of *all* combat elements: infantry, artillery, air support, tanks, reconnaissance, communications, intelligence, supply, and transport. Those colonels who appreciate the interrelation between elements in warfare are moved to this level, and the Army sends them to the War College in Carlisle, Pennsylvania, to get ready for it.

In a university an analogous variety of elements requires coordination and management. With the contemporary proliferation of subject-matter specialties, most institutions of higher learning keep a lookout for individuals who show a knack for bringing disparate academic efforts together. Such persons become increasingly valuable to large, multipurpose institutions. They not only engender the collaborative, cooperative incentives in otherwise isolated faculty loners, but by harnessing several specialties together, they help break down the parochial, closet mentality of the old-line disciplines. The academic cost benefit of all this comes as a further pleasant

13

surprise. New avenues of research are opened up, new intellectual friendships are cultivated between hitherto segregated faculties, and new job opportunities for students are created.

Because of the high demand for persons with this collaborative, integrative skill, some professionals deliberately shape their careers toward multifield enterprises, discovering as they go along that in the tight soft-money market of the eighties, their broad-gauge undertakings increasingly win out in the competition against the old-style, high-resolution focus of the conventional research project. The philanthropic foundations and government-grant agencies seem more and more interested in interdisciplinary inquiry, and they open their wallets accordingly.

The interdisciplinary types are visibly at work these days on the nation's campuses. They develop hybrid fields like biophysics, bioengineering, and psychohistory. Sometimes they invent entirely new fields—American studies, urban sciences, black studies, women's studies, communication arts, criminal justice, gerontology, bilingual-bicultural education, ethnography—some of which survive as viable disciplines and some of which fade when political pressures subside.

If an individual is successful at managing these unorthodox combinations in the churning politics of a university campus, he or she may be cultivating those attributes that lead to deaning. Unfortunately, higher education in the United States has no equivalent of the Army's War College to train individuals for these kinds of responsibilities. However, as in other kinds of organizations, a demonstrated expertise in modest managerial combinations such as these is sometimes taken as a clue to potential success in larger enterprises. With the right blend of skill and desire, therefore, the academic colonel (department head) may wish to reach for a higher command as a brigadier general (dean).

Another requirement of the administrative temperament is what might be labeled a well-developed *tolerance for chaos*.

14

We read in psychology books about how some people are task-oriented. We are told that mental health is somehow associated with seeing things through and with experiencing periodic moments of achievement. Somewhere deep inside each of us, they say, is a desire for completion, a drive toward closure. It is altogether likely that this drive is not distributed evenly among the population, but there is no arguing that those of us who go into academic work tend to have a lot of it. It probably originates in our training. PhD degrees may be merely union cards to some people, but to those who have survived graduate school, it is a given truth that the socialization process of the typical doctoral program, whatever else it does, certainly intensifies the desire to get things done.

When the assistant professor moves into an academic position fresh out of grad school, he or she discovers, as expected, that the work itself is laid out to accommodate this closure orientation. A university's calendar is full of endings. Class sessions begin and adjourn; exams are given, graded, and returned; courses end and a final grade for each student is recorded in the registrar's office; terms terminate and students are graduated at year-end commencements. Not only that, but the professor's other work follows the same orientation. Committee reports are written, experiments are completed and their results recorded, articles are accepted and published, and—end of ends—federal funding stops! The phenomenon of closure completely surrounds us in academic life; it is perhaps more deliberately and institutionally provided for in a university than in any other kind of organization.

By training and habit the faculty seems attached to this regimen. There are always a few stragglers, but in general faculty members do get their grades in and do manage to clear their committee dockets in time for midterm break. Now it so happens that the individuals who aspire to or are seen fit for administrative work are among the most adept at living this kind of closure life. Indeed, it is their very adept-

15

ness that marks them as administrative prospects. They seem well organized, they turn in reports on time, they meet deadlines for the submission of teaching schedules and purchase orders, they have a knack for *follow-through*.

The anomaly is that administrative work is not like that. It runs on and on in an open-ended and seemingly endless list of problems that need solving. A few problems can be solved with a phone call, but the vast majority require rounds of consultation with other individuals, days, weeks, maybe even months of conferences, committee meetings, and memoranda to be brought to something resembling closure.

The university calendar, so close to the life of a professor, is only hazily perceived outside the faculty orbit. The beginning and ending of courses, the start or finish of a semester, the occurrence of vacations or holidays have little connection with the workload and therefore the career rhythm of administrators. The rhythm unit of a dean or higher administrator is the fiscal year, a long stretch of eon magnitude in the minds of most faculty. And fiscal years, although they do have formal endings—say, on June 30—tend in practice to blend into one another. For example, as the name implies, the primary concern of the fiscal year is the institution's budget. A fiscal year budget may be "put to bed," but that only means that the computer is ready to take a slice-of-life look at things at some arbitrarily chosen instant. The submission of a budget by some specified date is not a closure. It never means that all the problems have been worked out; it merely means that they are well enough defined to be postponed for further study in the succeeding budget. Budgetary problems are never really resolved; they are merely massaged, manipulated, and reshaped so they can be dealt with and managed in as creative a way as possible during the succeeding twelve months.

The same indeterminacy syndrome is true also of program design and review, another major work area of administrators. In most large universities and in many small ones, a program proposal that originates in a faculty group must

16

pass upward through layer after layer of review before it is finally ratified for formal start-up in some September. These reviews frequently result in the proposal being returned to the next lower level of review so that objections can be taken care of. Sometimes this "bumping" sequence lands the material back in the hands of the faculty who first promulgated it, possibly many months after it originally left their hands.

In this situation the administrator must become a broker working out a settlement acceptable to all parties. Like a labor negotiator, he or she may spend weeks or months running back and forth between contending parties in search of a solution that is, if not exactly harmonious, at least palatable enough to win 51 percent of the votes when the final tally is taken.

These negotiating phases can sometimes last so long that by the time a proposal is returned to the original authors, they may have changed their priorities or decided to do the same thing differently. Their spirits flag and they balk at further efforts at compromise. However, the administrator knows that the matter, for internal political reasons, simply cannot be dropped, and the search for resolution must go on. Interest in the original idea must somehow be revived and pumped up, and the parties forcibly brought together to once more push ahead. It is a long, cluttered road, and sometimes even though closure is finally obtained, everyone is too exhausted to enjoy it.

An administrator's task is not so much to get closures one after another, as to keep his colleagues believing that closures are possible and worth working toward. An administrator's mind-set is accordingly fastened to process rather than product, to the act of problem-solving rather than to solutions. The administrative temperament must therefore transcend the closure expectations learned so well at the faculty level. Even better, the administrator must learn how to get the experience of closure, achievement, out of his or her non-closure existence. It is an existence filled day by day with

17

committee meetings, memorandums, and consultations. But it is also an existence of helping other people—the faculty—move toward *their* closures. The individual with an administrative temperament can find genuine satisfaction in this kind of activity.

Understandably, the open-endedness of an administrator's work, no matter how well performed, is vulnerable to attack from those not attuned to a life without closures. To them nothing ever seems to get done. Although this may not be the case, especially when viewing an institution's progress and therefore an administrator's performance over the long run, nevertheless a dean is the natural target for the frustrations of those who demand closure experiences every week. The short-term rhythm of faculty expectations is accordingly always in a state of tension with the long-term epicycle of the administrator's institutional expectations. This means that another major feature of the administrative temperament must be what we will call *epidermal conditioning* or a toughening of the skin so as to withstand a steady tattoo of criticism from one's colleagues.

As noted earlier, there has grown up in American higher education a strong antipathy toward administrators. In many places it manifests itself in genteel teasing and friendly scorn for the seemingly unintellectual, and therefore allegedly undemanding, nature of the administrator's job. In other places it takes on uglier tones, leading to a Pavlovian, knee-jerk aversion and contempt for all things administrative in character, culminating in some individuals in a permanent state of ill-concealed disrespect for all ranks above full professor.

As a group, faculty members do not consider themselves hard to get along with. They are not inclined to entertain the possibility that they are strong-willed, now and then unreasonable, sometimes irascible and unpleasant, and on some occasions downright dishonest. Quite the contrary, faculty members view themselves as nice people who have deliberately chosen academic life as a career and thus proved that they have turned away from the obnoxious climbing, aggressive jungle behavior of their fellow citizens in the status-conscious worlds of free-enterprise commerce and government bureaucracy. This benign self-concept among university professors probably stems from a halo effect surrounding the intelligentsia in every society, namely, that since they are demonstrably more intelligent and articulate than their fellow citizens they must also be better as people, i.e., more sensitive, responsive, cooperative, and generous. Working from this non sequitur, faculty members find the surveillance of superiors uncomfortable, an insult to their sense of rectitude and motivational purity, and an institutionalized questioning of their niceness.

In the faculty's subconscious also lurks the notion that the work they do, teaching and research, is a kind of activity that does not require towering structures of organizational apparatus to make it work. An office, a desk, some bookshelves, maybe a typewriter, a few classrooms and laboratories, a library, and a schedule of hours thumbtacked to the bulletin board are all that are needed. In the faculty's view a university is the kind of place that can more or less run itself once the faculty and students are brought in touch with one another. Administrators, they believe, are superfluous, make-work bureaucrats who interfere with the main business of the institution and who, with their huge salaries, divert resources from what a university is all about.

Out of these companion, mutually supportive illusions—a self-concept of pleasant untroublesomeness and a job analysis of tasks needing little or no coordination and management—comes the widespread antiadministrator syndrome characteristic of most American institutions of higher learning. An administrator enters into his or her work with this attitude firmly in place and well established as a permanent condition of the environment. As they say, "it comes with the territory." No matter how manageable this attitude may be and no matter how much its effects may be ameliorated by artful handling of an institution's affairs, our long experience with it in colleges and universities in this country has resulted in an adversary relationship between faculty and administrator on the typical American campus.

So well conditioned are most faculties to this adversary outlook that they quickly socialize new faculty members into its tribal requirements, namely, a quick skepticism of an administrator's utterances and an automatic doubt about his or her motives. This attitude has, over the years, been given tacit endorsement by the American Association of University Professors, whose publications are heavily laced with antiadministrator sentiments. In fact, the adversary relationship is so well fixed in the association's corporate mind that it extends only associate, i.e., second class, membership in the association to those in administrative ranks.

For the new dean, who has in most cases just come from the "niceness" syndrome of the faculty and is as yet uncomprehending of the *real* job analysis that lies ahead, the intensity of this adversary relationship comes as an unpleasant surprise. The step to an administrative position is a passage from one social condition to another, almost like moving from one social class to another. To one's faculty colleagues, it is considered a changing of sides! Some years ago an individual moved from a professorship of English in a university in New York State to a major deanship of a woman's college in a large university in New Jersey. She found her shift to deaning sufficiently traumatic to warrant entitling her opening speech to her new faculty, "From Us to Them." It turned out to be a sensitive and moving statement, revealing beneath the well shaped rhetoric an individual with uncommon insights. But the very choice of such a theme also revealed that she felt it necessary, as her first believable credential, to explain to herself and to her new colleagues why she had made the move, what it felt like to desert one's class, and what new, unanticipated obligations she was prepared to lay upon herself in her new role.

This adversary condition is a feature of academic life with which every administrator must sooner or later come to terms. The grounds for dealing with it are probably to be found in those untested zones of character to which we turn in new situations. Like unused muscles they ache at first but then surprise us with their strength and resiliency. In the case of the academic administrator, they represent that combination of elements which suggests an at-ease sense of self, a healthy acceptance of who one is amid the jostling demands of university life, in short, a personhood with its illusions under control.

Once the administrator can declare these elements in place, he is prepared to accept the fact that he is viewed by the faculty as one who has "left his people" for administration. He is, as the anthropologists put it, the outsider!

Being an outsider exacts its penalties. For one thing, it represents the onset of a new alignment of one's social environment. For the first time, the administrator must learn to live an institutional as well as personal life, now functioning as an impersonal mechanism, a transmission box through which, in one direction, institutional expectations are articulated and, in another, faculty energies are transformed into usable services. In this state of organizational detachment, a dean discovers that what any individual faculty member wants— and some want it badly—may have to yield on occasion to what the institution, i.e., everybody else, wants. The art of administration consists partly in delivering an institutional no to a faculty member with the least grinding of gears in the transmission box. Understandably, the presence of the adversary relationship tends to complicate this transaction. Given the gear grinding on most campuses, it is safe to say that the "art" is still in a primitive state of development.

The outsider must pay one final price, the surrender of personal friendships among the faculty. Whether brought in from the outside or appointed from within the ranks, the administrator soon discovers that close ties with members of the faculty are no longer possible. It is not simply that adversaries cannot be friends; sometimes they can. Opposing lawyers in a courtroom or U.S. senators in acrimonious debate can leave their respective chambers arm in arm, have a drink, go to a party, and have a good time together. But they are horizontal adversaries, equivalent in rank and role, serving independent constituencies, neither having any jurisdiction over the other. In organizational hierarchies, this is not the case. The assumption of administrative responsibilities signifies that a new, vertical variable has been introduced into the mix, namely, power and subordination. No matter in what small amounts or in what mild strengths these ingredients are applied, their presence is inimical to the act of friendship.

As the above indicates, a tough exterior is essential, but it must be matched with a special kind of interior. We all know the quality signified by the metaphor *warmth*. In describing the interior of the administrator, we are looking for an antonym to this term, a word that unfortunately cannot be located in the English language. We will coin one and call it *coolth*.

The need to reach for a new term is prompted by a recognition that the available terms will not exactly do. *Coolness, aloofness, cool-headedness, detachment, distance*, all are not quite right. In search of the quality in question, it may be well to approach the quality indirectly.

An administrator is neither a monarch nor a president; but, as modest as it is, there is a sense in which it may be said that he or she "comes to power." Coolth has something to do with the grace of handling power. Coming immediately to mind is Ernest Hemingway's definition of presidential leadership, which John F. Kennedy was fond of quoting, "Grace under pressure." But leadership implies grace at other times too. It signifies a measured restraint in exercising power, a holding back and a measuring out of just the amount of power necessary to get the decision made and delivered to the affected parties to be put into action.

In our common lingo these days, as expressed, say, by TV entertainer Flip Wilson, the word *cool* stands for a quality not unrelated to what we're after here. In Wilson's lexicon, *cool* means being clever without ostentation, being responsive but cordially one-up, being *in* but always slightly *above* the situation at hand—a philosopher might call it being metasituational. To be cool in this sense is to have an easy ability to manipulate these variables toward some outcome that is better, if ever so slightly, than what went before—all accomplished with a passing good nature and without attracting attention.

Now, if we put all these ideas together, we can discern a feature of administrative temperament that contains multiple elements which seem to cling together. First, there must be a capacity for solid homework, i.e., getting all the variables in mind and clearly understood. It helps if one is a "quick study" capable of digesting reports and memorandums at a brisk Evelyn-Wood clip. Second, there must be a capacity for close, one-on-one understanding of individual members of the faculty. A skilled administrator allots considerable time to this, sitting down with them over coffee, engaging them in small and large talk. This is another form of homework, namely, listening closely to members of the faculty to learn what ideas appeal to them, what they like and do not like about their colleagues, what work they find most gratifying, and, most important, what they themselves want out of the organization beyond the customary rewards of rank and salary. In short, the administrator must be able to acquire a personal knowledge of individual faculty members without knowing any of them personally! Finally, the administrator orchestrates these elements—without flourish or a raised voice—pushing here, complimenting there, rearranging options as more individuals are consulted, and eventually bringing the elements and individuals to a culmination that will be seen as opening up new and more personally satisfying spheres of activity for those involved.

Through all of the above, there is the strong suggestion of a low profile. It is probably true that an administrator can afford a modicum of flamboyance in some sectors of the job—e.g., in talking with reporters or peddling projects in Washington, D.C.—but not in the day-in-day-out management of people and ideas. This area requires being discreet, evaluating semipersonal information, and sometimes holding confidences. Moreover, administrators are expected to maintain a tight rein on their emotions. Faculty members are permitted to lose their tempers, break down in tears, call each other names, and insult the dean covertly or publicly. This license does not extend to deans, however, even under the most outrageous of provocations. Free speech applies to faculty members, not to administrators. The quality of coolth therefore implies a steadiness of mood, a controlled repose under pressure, a mental orientation to tomorrow and next week in the face of this afternoon's setback.

As the above implies, coolth also suggests a readiness for anonymity and a willingness to be ignored when credits are handed out. One of the necessary paradoxes of the administrative temperament is that a dean must bring a sturdy ego and hearty self-confidence to the job but must at the same time be willing to bury those attributes to bring closure to a problem. The price for closure is simply this: the ideas enabling closure, even the dean's own—especially his own—must be credited to the faculty if they are to be successfully implemented.

Deanly leadership, therefore, presents a special psychological burden. Although football teams recognize their need for quarterbacks, academic faculties perpetuate the fantasy that they succeed more or less on their own. A dean must be able to live gracefully with that untruth.

\* \* \*

Central to an understanding of the managerial art is an understanding of the faculty, that group of individuals for whom the administrative temperament is cultivated and developed. The faculty represents not only a workforce to be governed but a political constituency to be served. In a university, mood, morale, and ambiance are central to an administrator's effectiveness. The dynamics of faculty politics are a lesson every administrator must learn well and quickly.

# THREE

# The Faculty and Its Politics

UNIVERSITY PROFESSORING is one of those occupations
toward which the general public exhibits an uneasy ambivalence. On the one hand, anti-intellectualism has characterized the American tradition from the beginning. Centuries of frontier westering and decades of technological
pragmatism have given applause to the adventurer, inventor,
experimenter, builder, and doer. The professor, the quintessential opposite of all these, is viewed by the ordinary citizen
as essentially "out of it." On the other hand, a faint mystique
attaches to anyone who makes a living solely through the use
of the brain. The badge of the intellectual, the PhD degree,
still awakens an unmeasured awe in the majority of lay citizens. They sense that somewhere in the vast complexity,
high science, and sophisticated ingenuity of the American
system, someone must have been in charge of thinking. This,
they surmise, is what university professors do at work.

Whatever its public standing, college and university teaching continues to attract a lively and dedicated group of individuals. They train for it at great expense in time, money,
and effort because they enjoy the act of thinking itself and
the ancillary task of bringing others to this same enjoyment.

Moreover, they come to teaching as a career because they find in it satisfactions not offered, they believe, by other lines of work. Teaching does indeed provide a work situation that is wealthy in what the psychologists call psychic income. Don't listen to those who voice the cliché that they went into teaching because they like to work with people. They went into teaching because it is one long ego trip. Except for show business and politics, no other occupation is so consistently conducive to a sense of self importance as teaching. It is a flattering, heady experience to have in front of you—every day, every week, for nine months of every year—an audience of individuals who want to learn something you already know.

In a well ordered catalog of occupations, it could even be argued that teaching is a specialized form of show business, since it provides a virtually limitless vehicle for self-expression and self-revelation. For the ham or pro, the classroom is a stage. Some professors enjoy flashing their intellects before an eager crowd. In their improvisational theatrics, they delight in fondling ideas and concepts, manipulating them into new combinations and fresh insights, to the mesmerized admiration of their students. Other teachers are invigorated by the soapbox atmosphere, where they can harangue their social ideology before a docile and accepting gallery of listeners. They use the classroom as a miniature political rally. Still other professors have a need for emotional exhibitionism, roughly equivalent to what Norman Mailer refers to as the politician's "unholy if curious passion to expose oneself."[1] Such teachers like to sit in a circle and first-name it with their students, believing that unloading one's hangups and agonies in a sense-y feel-y session is the pathway to pedagogical authenticity.

Thus, there is no question that the classroom is a rich and versatile medium, serving as the professor's proscenium, stump, or encounter group.[2] And teaching has an ultimate

[1] "The Search for Carter," *New York Times Magazine*, September 26, 1976, p. 69.

[2] Some people, sad to say, go into teaching, as into police work, to lord it over other people. They are exhilarated by the teacher's psychological power position,

advantage over other media: unlike politics and entertainment, new audiences keep coming even after you've lost your stuff!

Overall, college teaching is a satisfying life. Especially with our present epoch's emphasis on self-definition and individual fulfillment, it is a line of work the academic secretly knows to be more personally rewarding than are the rat-race pursuits of others in the so-called "outside world." Considering the *angst* of the age—with so many searching for personal meaning in a routinized society—it is a secret worth keeping. Whatever else it is, college teaching is not routine, and the professor knows he has a good thing.

A look at the professor's daily schedule may help to account for this. Unlike employees in other kinds of organizations, a university professor performs much of his or her work in a condition of self-imposed solitude: reading, writing, and thinking are solitary activities. Even in the act of teaching, the professor is, from an organizational standpoint, operating alone, cut off for fifty minutes from the remainder of the institution. It is virtually an article of faith that in the classroom, the professor is absolutely sovereign.

Moreover, a professorial day's work is driven by well understood incentives. The gifted teacher or tireless researcher is devoted to the attainment of clear objectives, namely, the perfect classroom performance or the definitive book in the field. Although giftedness in teaching and scholarship is distributed unevenly, it is still true that these aspirations represent the pole toward which professorial motivations generally vibrate. They constitute the career orientation that explains what a professor's strivings are all about.

It so happens that the reward system of a university, unlike that of other organizations, has an extraterritorial dimension. Although not so true of teaching, a professor's reputation as a *scholar* is not established within the institution, but

---

and they use the classroom as a mental concentration camp to humiliate, ridicule, and abuse their students, thus working through their own feelings of inadequacy.

rather among a national audience of peers and subject-matter confreres. Hence, rising in the organization—almost a given anywhere else as a spur to performance—does not operate with uniform consistency in a university setting. Since the psychic rewards the professor seeks originate elsewhere, they must be imported, modulated, and processed into convincing entries in a promotion dossier; only then are they converted into concrete rewards within the organization. It is therefore necessary for the aspiring professor to make a career of playing to this external gallery at conventions, conferences, and through the learned journals. Once acclaim has been obtained there, it can be brought home and fed into the promotion mechanisms of the university and bartered for the hard goods of rank and salary.

Understandably, some individuals are more imaginative than others in designing and constructing their image outside the university. They bring to their professoring a public relations artistry, a feel for the hot topic. They come to a university career with undisguised notions of becoming famous. They see themselves headed for the cover of *Time Magazine*—another Salk, McLuhan, Galbraith, or Skinner. They fantasize being on TV talk shows with Carl Sagan, Milton Friedman, or Ashley Montague. And if these extravagant dreams eventually seem out of reach, ambitious professors then aim at national visibility within a specialty. But even this must be carefully programmed and managed year by year on the national stage so that the external applause makes the loudest noise within the organization, specifically to a professor's senior colleagues from whom the recommendations for promotion eventually have to come.

As we shall see later, the promotions system of a university can be trivial or elaborate. In some places, it can become divinely bureaucratic, with the carefully worded dossiers working their way slowly up the ladder, committee by committee, to some ultimate decisionmaker on the top floor. But whatever its design, a promotions mechanism comes down to this: it is the institution's way of perpetuating itself in its own image. It is the medium through which the institution's ethos is recharged and reborn with every generation of new PhDs. If one learns the counters the institution values most—teaching, research, service to the community, general usefulness around campus—it is not difficult to orient one's skills toward those activities that yield the greatest payoff. It is not so much a matter of outsmartng the system as of understanding the system, accommodating one's motivations to it, and making it work in one's favor.

For a few professors, those perhaps too good at the promotion game, an unusual occupational hazard lies in wait. They pursue their careers, rising quickly to the rank of full professor before, say, forty, continuing to develop their teaching skills, cultivating a coterie of protégés in doctoral programs, and cranking out articles and books. Then, after twenty years of this, they wake up one morning with the uneasy sense that the steam is running out of their ideas. They have pushed their creative faculties about as far as they can be made to go. It is said that mathematicians burn out at thirty, physical scientists at forty, and social scientists at fifty. Only novelists and philosophers can keep on rearranging the universe into their sixties and seventies.

Also, being around young people too long can be debilitating. The new PhD getting that first job has high hopes of staying young. What better way than to plan a career so that you are always surrounded by youth? The professor gets older, but the students remain the same—always in their late teens or twenties. What an exhilarating prospect to work with fresh minds all the time!

A special, not uncommon and somewhat melancholy, case of this syndrome is the "flaming liberal" who leaves graduate school, PhD in hand, fighting for a cause, attaching himself to every ideology embraced by young people, and fully expecting to identify with his own studenthood forever and ever. On his first job this individual deliberately cultivates iconoclasm as a lifestyle, knowing that mischiefmaking on behalf of student causes is immune from institutional discipline. To preserve his identity, he floats himself on the surface of each new cause. He is considered by the students ideologically as one of them, but he is used by them as faculty "point man" for dialectical boat-rocking with the establishment. Sooner or later he discovers that, politically speaking, students represent the weakest constituency in the university (except for the secretarial staff) and that his perpetual posing as a student is ludicrous.

Whatever the motivation, the bloom-of-youth argument begins to wilt as the academic gets into mid-career. Like the first-grade teacher who begins to talk like the six-year-olds, the university teacher discovers that he or she is starting to talk like—or, worse, to think like—the college kids and grad students on campus. At thirty this is probably good, but at forty-five, it is bad. Innocence has its charm, but, as with other things, one can have too much of it.[3]

For the great majority of professors, of course, the mid-career disenchantment with peaking too early never comes. They haven't peaked. They struggle on, year after year, well into their fifties with only modest records of teaching and research to show for their efforts. Some of these individuals come to accept the unpleasant truth that intellectually, they just don't have it. Showing early promise and initial achievement, they have advanced to tenured status. But with con-

[3] Cynthia Ozick, in her story, "The Laughter of Akiva," (*New Yorker*, November 10, 1980) offers a touching, poignant description of this phenomenon. Karpov is the headmaster of a private elementary school in the East. One day he enters the first-grade room to engage a child in conversation in arithmetic: "The tender head stayed down. The child did not reply. He took in, with no reservations, that she was not one of the bright ones, and just then the pang, the sensation, the almost-animal that ran its warm paws alongside his liver, made him know again his condition; his discovery. His condition was immortality. . . . year after year it was the same, the first graders so tender-mouthed and little, the eighth-grade girls exploded into puberty, the candle-tips of their breasts puffed up beneath their white dresses in the long procession up the glowing hill; spring after spring after spring. Nothing moved. Nothing altered. The first grade always the first grade, the eighth grade always the eighth. This knowledge turned him cold; it was the coldness of the cosmos itself. The same, the same, the same. Nature replaces, replaces identically, replaces chillingly. . . . he was dying of unchangingness; he was dying of lack of death— . . . he could not dream the end, no one grew old for him."

tinuing application, their work somehow dies, never reaching recognition, either in-house or outside the university, to warrant advancement to a full professorship. They finish their careers as journeymen, teaching basic courses, publishing an occasional article, and having personally come to terms with the prospect of reaching retirement still at the rank of associate professor.

Out of these feelings a self-serving bitterness can easily develop. The losers contend that the journey to a full professorship is agony, a game played by rules that are misdirected and phony. The heavy emphasis on research and publishing still prevails in most of the nation's better universities. To these individuals, convincing colleagues year by year of the cleverness of one's ideas is a pointless and degrading enterprise. To them it leaves out of the accounting other professional talents of great value to a university such as the ability to explain other people's ideas or the personal warmth necessary to make a nervous sophomore begin to grow. The human condition, they argue, is not just in the cranium but in the whole person, and the institution suffers if it does not remember this.

A separate word is necessary concerning another group, a special class of individuals who, for unknown reasons, seem unable to organize their lives for first-rate academic performance even though they appear to have the necessary intellectual equipment. In private conversations, in informal seminars, in departmental committee meetings, these persons reveal a depth of insight, a keen analytical ability, and a fundamental inquisitiveness, all of which should go into the making of a solid scholar. But over months and years disappointingly, nothing ever comes from these fine minds except vague comments about having "gathered lots of material on that idea" or imprecise promises about "putting those data together into publishable form." These individuals are an exasperation, a mystery, to a university dean. They represent a lost resource, a tantalizingly rich vein of original ideas no one knows how to reach. Maybe they moonlight too much and run out of energy at the office, or they may be distracted by troubles at home. Barring these possibilities, they must suffer from some undiagnosable form of *scholar-block*, a psychological interference that intrudes between mind and typewriter.

This phenomenon has no easy explanation, except perhaps a gloss on the conditions of academic work itself. We discussed earlier how much of the professor's life is spent alone, with books or students. For those professors not comfortable with solitude and not inclined to play to the external gallery of refereed journals, the environment of intellectual stimulation is confined to the institution itself—that is, to their students and their faculty colleagues. Even among this population, however, a selective factor is at work. The professor seeks out for his or her own stimulation only those who are intellectually comfortable and personally congenial. This means, therefore, that a professor's chances for growth, intellectual and professional, are eventually determined by what he or she chooses by way of academic colleagueship.

Personal discipline also has a lot to do with it. An environment of stimulation is defined partly by how diligently one devotes himself to reading and study. The whole library, all two million volumes, sits waiting. But how much of it is examined, pored over, plumbed for new insights is a professor's own decision.

The finish of a doctoral program is often followed by a heavy let-down, amounting in some people to an overt disgust with formal education. Counting kindergarten, the PhD has spent twenty years going to school. Here one is, twenty-five years old and a third of a lifetime gone, with nothing to show for it except report cards, term papers, and a forgettable dissertation. At this point, a malaise of the spirit hits almost every individual who has decided to make a career of university teaching.

Like all despondencies, this one will eventually go away. But when? For those PhDs who go into industry or government, it recedes rather quickly. On their first job, they become employees in the literal sense, which means that their jobs are defined for them. Moreover, their work assignments are significantly different from those encountered in twenty years of schooling. But for the academic, taking the first position as an assistant professor is to be plunged back into the very environment from which the sense of disgust and boredom originated. Although one is now on the other side of the desk—from which circumstance some excitement can be realized—all else is the same. Books, students, and teachers are all around. Talking, listening, reading, and writing are once again the entire medium of exchange. As before, words, words, words, and maybe a few numbers dominate the environment.

In returning to an all too familiar environment, the new professor requires a rejuvenated eagerness in order to locate those centers of stimulation from which postdoctoral growth can begin. And the new PhD soon learns, after the flush of pleasure over the new job has subsided, that postdoctoral growth is what is expected in the years ahead. He or she now lives among highly educated people for whom the PhD degree is, in retrospect, considered merely a necessary nuisance on the way to a university post. The new appointee is once again a freshman, surrounded by condescending upperclassmen. To succeed in this quasi-hostile subculture, the new professor must grow and develop far beyond the understandings obtained at the doctoral level.

\* \* \*

These, then, are the conditions of the craft: an indifferent public, a classroom audience wishing to be entertained, a scholarly audience somewhere out there beyond the campus asking for new truths, and within the institution a rigorous intellectual "beauty contest" always in progress in front of tough, demanding judges. But one more feature of academia requires special comment, since it helps us understand the political life of a campus, namely, the freedom under which academic work is conducted.

An academic career is what one makes it. As an occupation, especially when compared to others within organizations, university professoring is unusually free of constraints, opening out to a broad span of personal possibilities. Few occupations can match it in offering a lifetime's opportunity to define oneself. But university professoring is carried on in a kind of freedom that many people cannot stand. Precisely because of its limitless array of possibilities and lack of rules, it can generate introspective doubts and corrosive insecurities in some people.

In a university a high premium is put on self-starting movement, on the ability to take charge of one's professorial life and routine. The professor is expected to work by himself, without direction or surveillance, not only in planning and executing classroom lectures and demonstrations, but more importantly in carving out over the years a special zone of scholarly inquiry sufficiently unique to call one's own. The sources of intellectual stimulation are self-chosen, the diligence of preparing for classes is self-generated, and the discipline necessary for years of reading, study, and scholarly research is self-imposed. The freedom of the professor, so well advertised and argued for in academic circles, however, comes at a stiff price: it is granted by the university in return for discipline, responsibility, and personal initiative in pursuit of academic goals—in short, in return for a level of maturity and self-direction befitting a free searcher after truth.

In universities, as elsewhere, political behavior is what one turns to when the openness of the environment becomes oppressive and threatening, when the possibility for things not going one's way appears for the first time as real. This behavior manifests itself in different ways: some of it healthy, affirmative, and *pro bono collegio*; some of it negative, destructive, and almost pathologic in character.

If it were not for the healthy political activists among the faculty, nothing would get done and no institution could grow and flourish. These individuals contend with the openness of their environment by making friends among their

34

colleagues and by building intellectual relationships through-out the campus. When they have a new idea to peddle, they try it out on other professors, take them to lunch, go out for a drink together. In these preliminary conversations they, like all politicians, build into their own plans enough ideas of other professors to bring them around as allies and con-federates. Later they openly lobby for support, carefully lay-ing the groundwork for a favorable vote from each member of the committee that will hear their proposition. It is a tru-ism in academic life that the cultivation of a single favorable vote may require months, sometimes even years, of the most artful stroking of the professor in question.

Eventually the homework pays off. The plan sails through, the undertaking is set in motion with new funds, new people, new office space, and new commitments from the university's officers. From this mode of politicking, everyone gains and the institution benefits.

But university politics have a negative face also; and, al-though this aspect is more depressing to report, this dark side of professorial conduct also occupies time and thought of a university dean. As noted, a university makes heavy de-mands upon maturity and self-direction. Many professors buckle under this load. They enjoy the freedom in which they work, but they are unable to deliver their part of the agreement. Some have deep insecurities about their capaci-ties as intellectuals. They turn to political maneuvering as a compensatory device to direct attention away from their pro-fessorial disabilities. Others, even those who are secure and successful, have doubts about unbridled libertarianism. They champion it for themselves but not for everybody else. They reach out for mechanisms of order that they can impose on their fellow professors and themselves so that lines can be drawn to define what is permissible and what is not.

It may begin in seemingly benign ways. Indeed, the politi-cizing of the university's business is natural and routine, un-dertaken merely to bring system and regularity to otherwise chaotic elements—a committee convenes, say, to decide on course prerequisites. But in these situations, one soon learns not only how things are decided but also the strength of one's own voice in having them decided one way or another. What starts out, therefore, as straightforward participation in decisionmaking can soon advance to another more mischievous level, namely, exerting one's weight for the pure pleasure of doing so. Here political behavior begins to take on a life of its own, exhibiting at this primitive level merely a trivial pettiness that, although not premeditated, can do serious damage. It is difficult to illustrate this kind of conduct. The following, drawn from what must distressingly be called real life, will have to stand as a prototypical example.

A professor, long known for her interest in environmental questions, brings to the campus senate a well thought out proposal for the establishment of a university center on ecological studies. More or less on her own over the preceding six months, she had cultivated possible funding sources, both public and private, to launch the center, and she is ready to go with a seed-money foundation grant of $100,000, pending senate approval. In the course of the discussion, an argument develops as to the role of students in this undertaking. One senate member in particular becomes agitated and ten minutes into the debate rises and makes an impassioned, populist speech on behalf of the students, arguing that the young have the most at stake in environmental quality and, for that reason, should be given a share in the administrative control of the center, this to be arranged by seating them on the center's proposed governing board. A heated exchange develops focusing on whether their voting privileges shall be equal to or only half that of the professors on the board. Thirty-five minutes later, the senate as a deliberative body decides to table the motion to approve the project and to defer further consideration of the proposal until the next year. Upon learning of this action, the foundation withdraws its offer of $100,000, and the professor's project is, for all intents and purposes, dead.

Sometimes the mischief is not so inadvertent, and we witness the emergence of another level of political behavior, namely, an organized attempt to obstruct. Here one sees the first tendency for faculty to choose sides. Whatever the issue, coalitions of faculty members now see that it is possible to control events and, depending on the situation, to advance their own hegemony in academic matters and to restrict the freedom of others. Here again examples are abundant but difficult to relate. Let the following be a paradigm sample.

A department wishes to develop a new program, but it announces that it does not choose to share the planning or operation of it with anyone else. However, a second department is interested in the program and, indeed, has some professors trained in the proposed area and eager to work on it. After some months of inactivity, with no planning coming out of the first department, the second department grows impatient and outlines a plan for its own professors to get to work on it forthwith. This development arouses the first department, provoking worries that their lack of interest in the program may mean they will lose jursidiction over it. Moreover, they are jealous of recent achievements of the second department, and it now becomes a political imperative to block the initiatives of this upstart group. They begin a systematic round of political caucusing with individual members of the committee charged with deciding the jurisdictional question. One of them intimidates a junior member of the committee, implying that if that person does not vote "right" on this issue, that person can expect no support for a research proposal in preparation. With this and other more sophisticated forms of arm-twisting, the first department succeeds in putting together a five-to-four vote margin in the committee to block the request of the second department to move ahead on the program.

The above illustrations bear overtones of raw power. But from a dean's perch, it is easy to see that an academic community abounds with hidden agendas also. Genteel filibusters can slow down an uncomfortable idea; a project can be "studied" for years. Sometimes deft monkeying with parlia-

37

mentary process can clog the machinery; a surprise quorum call at notoriously underattended faculty meetings is a favorite stratagem. These measures failing, more subtle tactics may be called into play. In committee meetings or in larger faculty meetings, articulate and imaginative professor/politicians will engage in inventions of dissembling that they would never tolerate in their own scholarship.

In the mid-seventies, Michael Maccoby, a student of organizational behavior, reported on a study of managers and professionals in different work settings. About university people, he had this to say:

> Although academics consider themselves more "humane" than businessmen, the engineers and managers we interviewed are no more competitive and a lot more cooperative with one another than most professors. If corporate managers engaged in the nitpicking and down-putting common in universities, little would be created and produced. If managers treated their subordinates with the neglect and contempt common in the attitude of professors to graduate students, no one would work for them. These days, the talented jungle fighter probably has a much better chance for advancement in the university than in the corporate psychostructure.[4]

In episodes like those above, the intensity of faculty politics begins its slow corrosion of the human spirit. Left unchecked it starts to weaken that basic regard for one's associates which is the evanescent cement holding together a fragile academic community. To many new deans such conduct comes as a bewildering surprise. Of course, a university, like other organizations, is a very human place, and political jockeying for influence and status within a campus must be regarded as natural. What comes as a surprise is the extremity to which such behavior is sometimes carried.

It is reasonable to inquire then why faculty members go to such lengths to get their own way. Some observers pass it off with a wisecrack: faculty politics are vicious because the

[4] *The Gamesman* (New York: Simon and Schuster, 1976), p. 209.

stakes are so low! There is wisdom somewhere inside this jest. Faculty members know that their rewards are indeed spare and sparse. The general public has only an ambiguous regard for them. The pay is marginal when compared with that in the other professions. Moving up in rank has limited capacity to soothe, since outside the tight brotherhood of academia its significance is little understood. Thus even the successful intellectual knows that he or she is viewed by others as a marginal contributor to the social economy. What is left? All that remains is the struggle for influence within the institution. But so often this influence is voiced through the pettiest animadversions and exerted upon the most trivial variables of academic life. The administrative onlooker—a dean, a vice-president, a president—is aghast at the amount of time and energy full-grown men and women will expend on it. Nevertheless, these tiny poker chips of effect are all that's left to fight over. Man, like the animals, they say, is a territorial beast. In an academic ecology, this must be understood to mean that real estate is to be coveted and conquered sometimes by the square inch.

All of this is a vexing, unwelcome reminder that academic folk are, sad to say, not much different from other people. Otherwise bright, articulate, and intellectually the cream of society, they are nevertheless capable of an uncharitable, mischievous self-interest that seems somehow out of place in a hall of truth.

This feature of professorial behavior infects all levels of the institution, but it erupts most frequently within departments and colleges, the chief business areas of academic middle managers. Deans must understand this behavior and comprehend the motivations behind it, then with this knowledge design countervailing measures that will lift collegial relationships to a somewhat higher, more generous level.

There is no question that some of this behavior is generated simply by personal dislike for one's associates. Personalities differ, and it is to be expected that within any group of individuals who are forced together for institutional or cor-

39

porate purposes there will be some who are less easy to get along with than others. Thus some political one-upmanship and collegial arm-twisting can be accounted for by the personal antipathies or hostilities that spring up in a university faculty.

Also, it should be remembered that the voicing of opposition to an idea is a reflex action of any intellectual. It is of the very nature of academic life to take exception, to raise questions, to examine further, to explore more deeply. Those activities are the very stock-in-trade of the intellectual in the act of being an intellectual. Indeed, there is something faintly dishonest about not doing those things, since the search for truth depends upon free criticism and tough examination of every idea. When, therefore, a professor takes his or her mental tools to a senate meeting, it is to be expected that these tools will not be laid aside but actively employed in handling the institution's internal business. Furthermore, professors get tired of talking to students all the time. Sometimes they want to play to adults. The senate floor is a perfect forum for rhetorical display and analytical theatrics, the more remarkable if they demolish the pet project of a respected colleague.

But personal hostilities and public posturing cannot account for all of the faculty's penchant for politicizing the internal workings of the organization. The intensity of some faculty backbiting comes from a deeper place. It is born of a fear and distrust of a colleague's values. In this sense, it is more literally political—as a politician uses this term—in origin and motivation. Our attitudes toward political candidates are shaped by forces stronger than personal likability or oratorical style. They are shaped by the politician's value-set, by his angle of approach to society's problems, by his leftness or rightness, his compassion, his estimate of his fellow man. University professors likewise take the measure of their colleagues not just on how bright, amiable, and cooperative they are, but by the values they hold and how they want those values to drive the work of their university.

40

In the late sixties and early seventies, the number one issue on most campuses was race, specifically on what to do with poorly prepared black and Latino students coming from intellectually impoverished homes, neighborhoods, and high schools. On every faculty, as in the wider society, there are irreducible numbers of what must be called guilt-burdened, white liberals. Then, as now, they pleaded for the compensation of minorities to atone for "four hundred years of oppression." They argued for opening up the "white man's universities" from which blacks and Latinos had been excluded, for wiping out "discriminatory" admissions policies, and for giving special assistance to inner-city—read "black and Latino"—citizens. In many places their guilt was co-opted by black and Latino students, leading to student-faculty groups being organized to intimidate university deans and presidents whose own guilt was toyed with and manipulated by hostile, militant sit-ins in university offices.

In contrast, at the other end of the spectrum were those who believed in, and still believe in, a meritocracy. They held to the old standards of universities down through the ages, chief of which is that only the brightest shall be educated at the university level. They viewed with alarm the erosion of admissions standards, the winking at academic requirements, the inflation of grading practices, all in the name of what they considered a misdirected form of social justice. Softening the requirements for minorities, they argued, is the most virulent form of racism.

On most campuses in the early seventies, these two groups locked horns. Each feared the other would take over the university and permanently direct it along lines of its own ideological choosing. Departments of sociology and philosophy have seemed especially hospitable to and a breeding ground for the white liberal; departments in the natural sciences and engineering have typically stood at the other end of the continuum, remaining meritocratically hardheaded about traditional university policies. But, wherever the pockets of ideology coalesced and hardened, they came to represent threats to the viability of the modern university, especially in the urban areas, in coming to terms with the awakened consciousness of the American polity. Faculty members lined up on every issue, determined to interpret the outcome in racial terms and weighing the consequences of proposed policies in terms of whether their own conception of the university would be furthered or foreshortened.

The late seventies and eighties have engendered a new set of arguments with a value base. Campus protests still aim at alleged institutional racism but now appear to locate that evil in extramural phenomena. Does the university invest its endowment in the economy of South African nations? If so, the symbolism of that investment is challenged and the faculty begins to choose up sides.

The eighties are destined to bring to a head one of the most explosive arguments yet encountered. It can be stated in terms of blunt options: shall there be a State of Israel or shall there be oil for the cars of America? As the Middle East continues to boil, the naked force of this collision has still to be felt. But it is inevitable that the academic community will one day be asked for its moral judgment on this question. Already, the University of Southern California has been forced to abandon plans to establish a Center for Arab Studies—certainly a move in keeping with our pluralist ethic—because of student and faculty protests that it would have been paid for—as it would have—with Arab oil dollars. If this can be regarded as an omen for the eighties, what more strenuous struggles lie ahead on the politics of oil? The antagonism and hostility that this confrontation will generate are almost too ugly to imagine.

\* \* \*

A university, unlike other social and economic institutions, is especially vulnerable to ideological politics. In other organizations, political persuasions are likely to be more homogeneous, tending to hover around the ambiance and focus of the organization itself; militant social activists do not get jobs in banks. In a university, however, everything is possible. Every political view, from far right to far left, is legitimate. Robert Frost used to define home as where "they have to take you in." Likewise, a university is the mind's home, and no matter how outrageous or unconventional an idea, a university is expected to find room for it. Thus, variety of idea is not just "the spice of life" to a university; it is a necessity. You cannot be driven out of a university just because of what you think.

But there is a final feature of ideological politics that explains its viciousness: ideologies are non-negotiable! Like religions, they cannot be discussed, only felt and expressed. For centuries, academic faculties have prided themselves on providing "a free marketplace of ideas." There is something about the human mind that enjoys the tugging and hauling of cognitive elements. Debate, disagreement, discussion, dialogue, the weighing of opposing bodies of evidence all are ingredients of vigorous and exciting intellectual life. Professors can sit around a seminar table, literally for hours, in the most heated exchanges concerning ideas, finally walking away with warm satisfaction that they have learned and grown as a result of the experience.

But the human system, in a professor or anyone else, is not capable of the same kind of tough exchanges regarding political and social ideology. Here the emotional structure of the individual gets involved. Values that have taken a lifetime to develop are attacked and threatened, and the very integrity of one's person is brought into question.

Some years ago, an education dean in an urban university established what he called the Brown Bag Forum, a Friday noon, bring-your-own-lunch discussion session in the dean's conference room. The purpose was to share views on the direction of the college, on its posture on social questions and its response to urban concerns regarding race and social class in the city's schools. In short, the intention was deliberately to

43

provoke a discussion among faculty and students not about ideas but about social sensitivities, ideological orientations, and personal commitments regarding the outside world.

After a few sessions, troubling tensions developed. It appeared that what was designed to bring the college community together was tearing it apart. Hostility, recrimination, name-calling and general verbal violence seemed increasingly to be the fall-out from each session. Finally, the discussions were abandoned, the dean in question having concluded that apparently there was no such thing as a "free marketplace of ideologies," at least not in the same sense that there can be free and open discussion of ideas. And that is probably because ideas are or can be made to be impersonal, whereas ideologies are by definition personal in structure. One's own personal structure is not open for discussion. It can only be lived with, and enjoyed or suffered.

The lesson in all of this for middle managers is easy to articulate but difficult to operationalize. First, there is an imperative to keep the lines of contact open between faculty members. The dean sits at the hub of the communications network and in that spot is capable of bringing individuals together on a continuing basis until jealousies are ameliorated or insecurities quieted. During the most intense and emotional of faculty fights, it is sometimes necessary to orchestrate these contacts with carefully selected third parties, for example, those faculty members who are not directly involved in the issue at hand but have an institutional interest in its amicable outcome.

Second, through continuing contact with individual members of the faculty, the dean can begin to discern those pressure points from which animus and hostility erupt. He or she is in a position to ease a proposal past these pressure points in a delicate way so as not to awaken unnecessary opposition. This means also, of course, that if hostility and opposition do develop, the dean will be ready with other options and alternatives as fall-back positions. Indeed, some fall-back options turn out better than the original proposal, precisely because

44

they engender fewer anxieties and summon up more wide-spread support from different factions of the faculty.

Finally, as the above implies, the openness of the dean's office itself can be used to set the tone for faculty interchange. It should be an easy place to go to when trouble lurks, not like a psychiatrist's couch but rather as a catharsis chamber where faculty members can sound off, venting their fears and hopes perhaps, but more important, articulating their problems as they see them, which is always the first step toward their solution. In an academic situation, the middle manager is the key officer in the hierarchy to make maximum use of this primordial material. Not only are these expressions of the faculty psychologically useful, but they also usually contain the clues for accommodation in getting on with institutional tasks.

Faculty members, like everybody else, are politics prone. But they are also colleague oriented. They do not want to live in a permanent state of warfare with their associates. The dean is in a position to cultivate this latter incentive.

# FOUR

# Salary, Promotion, and Tenure

IN A UNIVERSITY the middle manager is the fulcrum of the reward system. The metaphor is chosen cautiously, for a dean may sit at the center of the evaluation apparatus, but at the same time he or she must share with many others the leverage of decisionmaking when it comes to dispensing the hard goods of recognition—money, rank and a permanent contract. Once an individual has been appointed to the staff, faculty committees are especially jealous of their prerogatives in rank and tenure recommendations. But beyond these areas a dean exercises significant power in deciding who shall and who shall not receive the applause of the institution for a job well done. Over the years, therefore, the caliber of faculty that survives the annual judging process becomes an extended reflection of the dean's academic values. As time passes, the faculty tends to approximate that configuration of brains, talent, and personality which represents the dean's definition of what a college should be.

Working from within the organization, a dean is surrounded by institutional limits, many of which are beyond his or her control to modify. In a university situation, money is one of those limits. Yet, for all of its general scarcity, money is the one variable in which the dean can sometimes exercise the greatest leverage. Being on the margins of the economy, university professors have never expected to be paid generously. They did not opt for an academic career out of cornucopian visions of living well. Nevertheless, like everyone else in a consumer-oriented social system, they are profoundly affected by money. Even small amounts of it carry messages which no folder full of memoranda could convey. The allocation of salary money therefore must be approached as something of a dispenser's art. Even small pressures on the money spigot, in either direction, can generate meaningful signals.

At the onset of a person's employment, a dean's options are surrounded by an array of givens. The tenured faculty, let us say, have completed a search and found the individual they want. In approaching this person as a prospective employee, the dean knows that starting salaries for new PhDs at the assistant-professor level have not changed in relative position for several decades. They are somewhat higher than beginning salaries for public school teachers (BA degree), about equal to those for public service professionals (BA or MA degrees), somewhat lower than beginning salaries for engineers (BS Eng. degree), and considerably lower than those at the starting echelons of business and industry (BS or MBA degree).

Furthermore, in some universities the existence of a salary schedule limits the latitude of "first offers." In these places the entire schedule must advance for the starting salary category to advance. In other institutions having no schedule, the dean's room for movement may be somewhat greater. However, this freedom breeds its own mischief. The first-offer range tends to fluctuate upward year by year in response to the economy's general inflation, thus yielding each September what amounts to a "going rate" for new PhDs, a salary level that the institution hopes to keep competitive with comparable institutions. This salary movement eventually produces a "bumping squeeze" on the remainder of the payroll simply because salaries for individuals at higher ranks and more years of service do not respond as readily to inflationary pressures. Beginning salaries crowd upward, with those above making only sluggish advances. The net effect of this squeeze is that salary differentials between ranks begin to disappear. Thus, when an individual is promoted from one rank to another, a sizable salary increase is not possible lest it put, for example, a new associate professor at a salary higher than those already serving in that rank. Also, as the squeeze intensifies, the range of salaries within a given rank narrows, thus making it more and more difficult to recognize merit within a given range. Sometimes, of course, the case for merit is so clear-cut that an individual may be at the top of his or her range even with fewer years in rank than others at that rank. Indeed, sometimes it is necessary to recognize a faculty member's contributions with a salary higher than some of those in the next higher rank. Understandably, this practice stirs up turbulence in the community that may be difficult to quiet.

The solution to the squeeze phenomenon would, of course, be to gradually raise the salaries of the upper ranks more rapidly than the beginning rate so as to restore the stretched out range of salaries that used to obtain. However, this solution does not appear likely within the near future. It collides head-on with a political reality to which every middle manager must make an accommodation, namely, that a strong egalitarianism in the academic mentality says that in a period of severe inflation the lowest paid workers should be given the highest raises. So long as this sentiment remains strong in the academic community, the tendency for salaries to bunch up, from beginner to near-retiree, is bound to worsen.

From a purely theoretical standpoint, it might be argued that if the reversal of the squeeze phenomenon could be accomplished, it should be allowed to continue operating well beyond the status quo ante point so as to stretch out university pay scales even more. To illustrate this argument, in the seventies the average full professor's salary was approximately twice the starting assistant professor's salary. There is a real question in management theory whether this is a sufficient spread. For maximum psychological impact, especially for career employees over the long haul, a large organization must maintain a salary scale with high levels at mid-career and very high levels at end-career points, thus yielding a continuum that will provide for salary incentives of more or less equal strength throughout the entirety of the salary range from bottom to top. Failure to maintain such a salary scale is to allow the incentives to diminish as the individual moves into the potentially most productive years. Indeed, this tendency represents one of the basic flaws of educational economics over the last couple of generations. School systems, colleges, and universities have remained competitive with the private sector in starting salaries, but they have permitted their career-goal, top-of-the-range salaries to fall behind. Many capable individuals have left educational work in mid-career for just this reason.

If the ratio between full professors and starting professors could be raised from its present two-to-one to perhaps three-to-one or even higher, it would be possible for salary increments to take on once again the real, rather than token, significance they used to carry. An adjustment of this magnitude is certainly beyond the political capacity of a middle manager; it would require an institutionwide policy legislated by the board of trustees.

Leaving these macroeconomic questions to higher councils, the dean must operate in a tighter, more confined space, best illustrated, as we have noted above, in the first offer negotiations. Here is where the microeconomics of salaries is actually played out and where the primary counters soon become evident to both parties. First, of course, are the things other than the doctorate the individual can bring to the organization. Sometimes the applicant's special expertise or previous experience will warrant adding premiums to the base offer. Often the prospect will bring a salary history, in which case the most recent annual salary rate (whether full- or part-time) must be fed into the figuring. Finally, there is the overt competition of other offers.[1]

At this point the dean may enter a negotiating mode in which, depending on the desirability of the candidate, the dean may entice the prospect with a list of advantages other than salary that the prospect should keep in mind. The non-salary negotiating mode is especially important today, since affirmative action procedures have severely limited hiring officers in exercising discretion in salary bargaining. No longer is it considered good form to try to get the candidate at the lowest acceptable figure, a practice commonplace in American personnel procedures. Instead, unless there are pronounced differences in background and training, all candidates in a given year must be extended substantially the same salary offer. For a dean, in the heat of negotiating, to agree to an add-on in order to sign a reluctant candidate is to court trouble. Later on, some local or federal affirmative action officer may come in for an audit and want to know why Prospect A was hired at one figure but Prospect B came in at $500 more. An explanation that the "sweetener" was necessary to close the deal would, in all likelihood, not be acceptable, and a charge of discriminatory favoritism could be filed.

Thus, at the point of entry a dean has little room for movement. His or her prerogatives for dispensing salary rewards must wait to be exercised later on during the annual salary-setting season. In most institutions this occurs in the spring as a prelude to the submission of the college's asking budget for the succeeding fiscal year, usually July 1 to June 30. Of course, in institutions in which salary increases are dictated

[1] During the sixties and early seventies, salary premiums were paid to minority-group individuals—blacks, Chicanos, Puerto Ricans, native Americans, white ethnics, women—to encourage greater representation of these groups in university faculties. These premiums were made necessary by the high demand and relatively inadequate supply of highly trained individuals from these groups, but these salary add-ons also stirred resentment among existing faculties as being basically unfair, representing money payments to individuals for their minorityness rather than for their professional or academic competence. To some individuals, they represent yet another example of establishment condescension toward these groups, a form of institutional racism and sexism not in keeping with the merit principle that should apply to all individuals.

50

by salary schedules, the dean has few decisions to make. But in those universities where faculty performance is closely monitored and where the merit system operates, individual assessment of each faculty member's performance over the preceding twelve months is the critical factor in deciding on salary increases. Customarily, the initial phases of this assessment are conducted by the department head, who is or should be much closer to the faculty member's professional activity. As we shall see later in this chapter, the criteria for the evaluation of faculty performance are summed up in the well known triad of teaching, research, and service. Although these three measures are customarily formalized for promotion and tenure considerations, they obviously apply also to the shorter span evaluations leading to salary determinations. It is on the basis of the department head's assessment of merit in these three areas that his or her recommendations for salary increases are made.

In recent years, the merit principle has been under some strain. During our current experience with severe national inflation, there has developed on many campuses a strong advocacy of the position that merit considerations should yield to across the board cost-of-living adjustments. That is to say, if there is to be an overall increase for the entire faculty, it should be distributed proportionately to all in accordance with the Cost of Living Index before any remainder is distributed on the basis of merit. Typically, during the seventies the annual salary-increase pool in the major institutions has not matched, let alone surpassed, the increase in the cost of living for faculty members. Accordingly, to permit cost-of-living considerations to become the first priority would be, in effect, to cancel merit as a deciding factor in salary decisions.

Some institutions have turned in this direction, hoping that merit allotments can be resumed when inflation subsides or is brought under control. Other institutions, fearful that inflation is now a permanent feature of our economy, have settled on a compromise, namely, to allocate perhaps half of the salary-increase pool to cost-of-living increases and the other half to merit increases. Still other universities have held steadfast to the merit idea, believing that, whatever the state of the economy, this is the only mechanism for rewarding quality and driving out dead wood and hópeless incompetents.

It is in this latter group of institutions, those holding completely to the merit principle, that we can discern an unexpected managerial benefit resulting from the otherwise grim fallout of an inflationary period. It may be explained as follows.

In these institutions, an average increase for the whole faculty may be set at 8 percent. However, the institution does not intend to distribute it in this fashion; instead, merit still controls. Thus, the faculty member doing an average job would receive 8 percent, resulting for that person in no change in real income. A superperformer would receive 12 percent, a figure the dean hopes the recipient will perceive as bigger than it really is. Finally, the least productive individual would receive no increase, resulting in a drop in real income.

In this configuration of options, the dean's leverage increases. It is now possible to cut salaries as well as increase them, an action that in noninflationary times would not be permitted. This new option thus expands the range of messages that can be sent. In an indirect way, it also makes possible a step-up in the volume of bad news to be sent to the slacker or incompetent, a pay cut usually carrying more psychological impact than a mere pay continuance. Inflation therefore yields a degree of managerial flexibility and leverage that earlier times did not provide. It is not a happy spot to be in, to arrange for the cutting of a salary. But in the hard realities of administrative decisionmaking, the dean needs a communication device that can send signals loud and clear. In an inflationary period, mere percentage points of salary increase assume this role.

\* \* \*

Beyond salary the faculty's most immediate concern is promotion. In most institutions a variety of ranks and titles are assigned to different functions within the organization. By custom, however, only four of these ranks are considered to be of faculty status: instructor, assistant professor, associate professor, and professor. The movement through this gamut to the final prize weighs heavily on most academic persons. As intended, it is the academic establishment's ritualized progression toward acceptance, a graduated gatekeeping mechanism to protect The Order.

As we shall see later, the rank of instructor is no longer as common as it once was, other rank designations having taken its place. For the most part today, an academic career begins at the assistant-professor level. In the major institutions, the holding of the highest degree in one's discipline is a prerequisite for appointment at this rank. Except for art, music, architecture, and a few other specialties, this usually means the doctorate. The prototypical initial appointment, therefore, is of an individual just out of graduate school with the PhD or EdD degree.

By custom and by protocols laid down many years ago by the American Association of University Professors, the assistant professor is given a six-year trial or probationary period, during which he or she must establish a record of achievement to warrant being retained indefinitely. In some institutions the individual's movement toward this goal is reviewed every year; in others a close look is postponed until the end of the third year. But in all institutions following A.A.U.P. guidelines, a mandatory review must be undertaken during the assistant professor's sixth year of service. At this point the record must be assayed in an "up or out" context. If the decision is favorable, the assistant professor is promoted to associate professor, usually with tenure. In a few special cases the individual may be given tenure without promotion. If the decision is unfavorable, the assistant professor is offered a seventh-year, terminal contract at that rank. By accepting this contract, the individual consents to termination of employment and separation from the institution at the close of the seventh contract year.

Since these decisions are usually made mid-way in the individual's sixth year, the terminated professor has approximately eighteen months within which to relocate. This extensive lead-time for job-hunting is perhaps the longest period provided by any organizational structure in the United States, certainly far longer than any comparable policy in the private sector. It manifests one side of a university's posture toward the individual, namely, a humanitarian interest in the loser, a feel for his or her integrity as a person. During the late seventies and into the eighties, when university jobs were hard to find, this humanitarianism was especially significant. Giving notice eighteen months in advance, however, also suggests a feature of academic management that is sometimes hard to explain to outsiders. If, over the course of six years, an individual is found ineligible to serve as a continuing member of the organization, how can one justify letting the unqualified person spend another year and a half practicing his incompetence on students and colleagues? No other profession would permit such a thing for more than a few months, and no business would permit it for more than a few weeks.

The explanation for this phenomenon—the glacial casualness with which an academic institution gets rid of the unfit—probably lies down deep somewhere in the intellectual's uneasy attitude toward institutional life. Unlike writers, artists, musicians, playwrights, actors, physicians, clerics, and most lawyers, academic people perform as functionaries in very large organizations. Although they do not like to be reminded of it, they are employees in a much more literal way than is true of other professionals. The organization, therefore, rather than the free market's demand for professors' services or their skill as self-employed entrepreneurs, becomes the primary medium of their security. Hence, every academic employee has a personal interest in seeing that the organization's axe is allowed to fall only with a jurisprudential sureness that the organization has acted rightly. In sum, university personnel policies are very much on the side of the individual, and the general faculty, through either compassion or, more likely, self-interest, see that they stay there.

But the matter goes deeper than that. The determination of fitness of a university professor is a highly subjective, uncertain art, especially nowadays when abilities other than getting published in the leading journals keep pressing forward for attention and consideration. Moreover, the judges, those tenured faculty members who sit on the tenure committees, feel a sense of responsibility for the loser's fate. Not only did they recommend the original appointment six years earlier, but by the protocols of most institutions, they have been held responsible for nurturing and shaping the individual over the years into a fully developed university professor. They cannot recommend terminating a colleague without simultaneously diminishing their reputation as predictors of promise in a newcomer and as wise mentors in bringing that individual to the full measure of his or her potential.

Thus, there is a great dragging of feet in the termination process. Termination is decided on only reluctantly, and it is usually postponed to the very last moment. In most places, there is even a genteel vocabulary that goes with it. Universities never speak of *firing* anyone. He or she is either *not retained* or *not reappointed*. His or her *contract is allowed to expire*, or the individual is *offered a terminal contract*, which offer subtly places on the individual the responsibility for deciding on the actual termination date. It is a ritual dance played according to the most careful music, most of it orchestrated years ago by the American Association of University Professors.

The overall question of how to define *fitness* in a professor is itself a subject of much controversy. As noted earlier, American higher education has come to settle on three primary criteria: teaching, research, and service.

Competence in teaching has traditionally been the most elusive and fugitive information to gather. For example, there is a continuing debate in the academic community as to how much weight one can give to student evaluations, subject as they are to irrelevant factors such as the grading policies or personal charisma of the instructor. Notwithstanding

55

the imprecision of such measures, most universities have, over the last decade or so, made formal attempts to obtain some index of informed consumer response to their teaching staffs. This is customarily done through carefully constructed questionnaires that students are asked to complete toward the end of a given course. Appendix A provides examples of how two Big Ten universities approach the student evaluation of teaching.

The category on teaching may also include skills at teaching-related activities such as course development, program planning, and instructional experimentation. An organized mind, a planning knack, and a daring to try out unorthodox teaching strategies are attractive credentials for a faculty member's promotion dossier.

Compared to teaching performance, a professor's productivity in research and scholarship is relatively easy to measure. There is, of course, the "page counting" syndrome so typical of the least sophisticated of faculty promotion committees. But since the length of a published article may not be a very accurate measure of its quality, such panels usually look further for evidence of substance. Was the article published in a refereed journal? Was the article originally a paper read at a conference? If so, was the conference program refereed? Was this paper invited rather than submitted? Has this article been cited by other scholars in their works? As for books, the panel may ask similar questions. Who is the publisher? What is the reputation of the publisher for books of academic quality? Has the book been reviewed? If so, let's take a look at the reviews. In all these ways the promotion panel can get a fix on peer-scholar judgment, sometimes even going to the trouble of soliciting ad hoc letters of review from scholars in the field.

The preeminent advantage of the researcher-scholar in the promotion game is that his or her work is quantifiable, in terms of bibliographic entries and total pages, and objectively judgable by experts in the given area. The output of the scholar is down in black and white. It is public and there-

56

fore is capable of being assessed and evaluated independent of the person who produced it. Partly for this reason, research and scholarship is the least vulnerable to attack as a standard for promotion, and in the better universities, it continues as the single most decisive criterion for advancement to higher ranks in the organization.

If teaching is relatively difficult to judge and scholarship relatively easy to judge, the category of service falls somewhere in between. This class of professional activity has two elements, namely, performance *inside* the institution, once termed for want of a better label *general usefulness*, and performance *outside* the institution in service to the community. The former can be evaluated by watching the individual perform both collaboratively with other faculty on committees, councils, and departmental groups and individually when asked to take on an institutional "housekeeping" chore of some sort.

The latter, extramural sphere of service presents more complicated and unfamiliar problems of assessment and evaluation. As we shall see in chapter 5, university relationships beyond the campus are vulnerable to highly volatile political groups. A faculty member, even with the best of intentions, can easily become entangled with these forces and come out the loser in the encounter. This brings discredit both to the individual and the institution she or he represents. But, more important, most universities are not certain when their faculties' involvements in the surrounding community are effective and when they are not. One measure, somewhat superficial in character, is public relations. Do the faculty member's efforts engender a more positive public image of the university? This can be measured by favorable comment in the public prints or in the electronic media. A second criterion is the concrete programmatic result of a faculty member's endeavors in the wider community. What programs—courses, workshops, conferences—have been initiated by the institution that can be directly traced to the faculty member's efforts? A final measure, but perhaps the

57

most difficult to document, is the degree to which the university itself has grown and learned from the faculty member's efforts. Is there a new understanding of the institution's educational role? Is there a heightened awareness of the university's commitment to its neighbors and of ways by which that commitment can be delivered on? Are there new research areas which have been opened up as a result of the faculty member's enterprise, and is that research under way? In all these lines of pursuit, the extramural service record of the faculty member can be documented for inclusion in the promotion dossier.

As the foregoing implies, there is general agreement that teaching, research, and service do indeed box the boundaries of a professor's work. But the actual determinants of excellence in these areas continues to elude most faculties. As a result, in some institutions, the redefinition of these three criteria is almost an annual event. Committees are routinely established to restudy these rubrics, what they mean, and, most important, what shall count as evidence of exemplary performance within each. Appendix B carries an account of how one university has fleshed out these categories.

Taking the three criteria collectively, it is to be expected that an individual faculty member will probably be more competent in one than another. This raises a managerial problem: should the three criteria, assuming accurate assessment can be obtained, be considered of equal weight in the final accounting? Institutions differ on this question, at least in intention, some declaring that the three are equal in importance, and others relating their weighting of the elements to the reputed "mission" of their institution. Can an undergraduate-oriented institution stress research at the expense of instruction for its students? Can a research-oriented institution be expected to serve the community? Can any institution do all three things well? Every faculty has its own answers to these questions. But floating above their public pronouncements is a hard reality, namely, it would be difficult, nay impossible, for any institution to fail to promote to associate professor an assistant professor who, in the six-year period, has established a "track record" of several refereed publications through his or her writings or research investigations. We have spoken earlier of national visibility, almost a catch-phrase among faculty when in the act of judging other faculty. It is this hard-to-measure recognition beyond the campus which keeps breaking through the surface of promotion conferences. Thus, in the final accounting, since the research and scholarship category, de facto, is the only viable avenue to this exposure, it always lands on its feet as the number one criterion.

The dean, by office and function, is assigned the primary responsibility for making these judgments. But since he or she cannot be everywhere and cannot know everything about each field within a college, it is customary to delegate to departmental committees and to promotion advisory committees the detailed analysis of the promotion dossiers that are to be considered for a given year. These groups then report to the dean with their recommendations.

However, the dean is not just an idle bystander. One of the first obligations of the middle manager in this activity is to see that the best possible case for each individual is developed by his or her department head. Procedurally, it is to the dean's ultimate advantage that every scrap of evidence, both positive and negative, be assembled. It is important also to make certain that what is assembled is, in fact, evidence. A promotion dossier cannot credit hearsay reports, rumors, or offhand judgments of colleagues or superiors. And, if reference letters either solicited or unsolicited are to be included in the file, it is expected that they will be signed by their authors.

When the dossier finally reaches the dean's desk, the weight of middle management responsibilities becomes noticeable. In these circumstances, a career is at stake, and that means that a person—with goals, aspirations, commitments, and involvements—is on the line. What to do with the committee's recommendation therefore takes on an element of urgency and seriousness not equaled elsewhere in the administrator's sphere of tasks.

59

If the committee's recommendation on an assistant professor is not to promote and therefore to terminate, the dean's response is more or less foreordained, namely, to concur. A working protocol in major universities is that administrators do not force unwanted individuals on their colleagues. If the senior faculty say no, then the administrator will only make trouble with a yes. Indeed, in some places it would be doubtful that the dean's affirmative in such an instance would carry much weight at the next level, unless there are clearly arguable, extenuating circumstances requiring such a reversal of recommendation.

If the committee's recommendation favors promotion to associate professor, the dean must then weigh a number of factors, chief among them, strange to say, is whether the individual in question is promotable to full professor. Does the dossier describe an individual whose momentum in the six probationary years is such that, with the passage of, for example, another six years, he or she will be ready for the top rank? If the answer to this is yes, then concurrence on the recommendation is called for. If there is any hesitation on this point, further study and reflection may be necessary. From a management perspective, it is not good leadership to encourage a faculty member who, one believes, cannot go all the way. American higher education is strewn with superannuated associate professors never likely to make it to the top. Some of them get stalled, some of them get diverted, but most of them should not have been promoted to associate professor in the first place. A vigilant promotions apparatus and a thoughtful dean some years previously might have been able to avoid the disappointment, heartbreak, and occasional bitterness of this last group.

The occasion for promotion from associate professor to full professor energizes the same panoply of consultations, dossiers, and evaluation panels, here confined to full professors. Another working protocol in higher education is that promotion cases must be acted on only by those at a rank higher than the faculty member being evaluated.

The criteria for the final promotion are formally the same as those cited earlier. However, at this juncture, the primacy of the research and scholarship criterion is further accentuated, with teaching and service fading in importance. To become a full professor in an institution of the front rank, one must demonstrate not only national visibility but a position of academic leadership in one's discipline throughout the nation. And, since again this demonstration is easiest to stage through one's writings and publications, the conferences of one's full-professor colleagues on whether to open the club to another member are heavy with articles, books, and the submitted judgments of learned referees in other institutions.

A dean's decision on a full professorship is understandably of far greater moment than that on lower ranks. For, besides honoring and recognizing a colleague with the highest award, the dean is also anointing the individual with advisory powers not accorded lower echelons. In many institutions the full professors constitute the middle manager's primary forum of consultants; collectively they serve as a sounding board for the dean's ideas, a tryout arena for projects and proposals before these ideas reach the formal infrastructure of committees, councils, and senates. Moreover, these groups at the campus level require the experienced, mature, and respected individuals, i.e., full professors, to serve on them. The individual winning the top prize can look forward to a heavy load of committee work throughout the university community. Accordingly, the step to full professor status implies pedestrian institutional obligations as a kind of penance for recognition of scholarly eminence. As most middle managers know, the *noblesse* is far easier for the new full-professor to accept than the *oblige*.

\* \* \*

Tenure is the least understood but the most jealously protected perquisite of academic life. The mandatory sixth-year review of the assistant professor is intended to yield an up-

61

or-out decision. In the leading institutions, the "up" decision to promote the individual to associate professor also carries with it indefinite tenure, a commitment of the institution to retain the individual in its employ until statutory retirement.[2] For some individuals who are fast starters, this can mean a stretch of thirty years!

From an institutional standpoint, therefore, the judgment on an assistant professor is far more critical than for any other person. At this decision point, the institution is not merely recognizing promise, but in fact purchasing an entire career. If mistakes are made here, the academic community must learn to live with them for a long time.

Many newcomers to academic positions mistakenly view their probationary years as eligibility periods, somehow thinking that each of the six years is a credit toward tenure. On the contrary, the nontenure years are explicitly probationary. The individual is literally on trial. The tenure apparatus is therefore not designed for the individual but for the institution. It is an apparatus whose purpose is to enable the institution over the years to define itself, to speak to the wider community as to what it is, what it stands for, and what expertise it shall be prepared to offer to the surrounding population.

The only deference to the individual is the judgment in some institutions that the six-year period is not long enough for individuals to prove themselves. This is particularly the case in those universities which require the doctorate as a condition for appointment at the assistant professor level, but in these institutions other complications develop. If the

[2] Historically, the only grounds for dismissal have been gross incompetence and something called "moral turpitude," some egregious violation of the community's moral standards. Since both of these are extremely difficult to prove, internally and in the courts, tenure rights are rarely tested. During the sixties and seventies, however, the courts acknowledged two new grounds for dismissal of tenured professors: (1) the elimination of a professorial position for lack of enrollment in that specialty and (2) threatened bankruptcy of the institution unless the departments with the lowest enrollments are shut down. However, these also are rarely used. For all intents and purposes, tenure means indefinite employment.

rank of instructor, let us say, is technically the bottom rung of the tenure ladder, an individual hired at that rank has six years in which to earn the doctorate and qualify for tenure. It is not difficult to see that this double task is probably asking for too much. In response to this, these institutions have attempted to remove the instructor rank from the tenure ladder or to employ individuals at other, nontenure ranks such as research associate, teaching associate, or often simply lecturer. With this stratagem, it is possible for these institutions to allow new appointees to come into the faculty but postpone their entry onto the tenure ladder until they are ready to do so, customarily at the point of the doctorate. In this manner an individual can be rehired every year with no obligation in either direction, and at a suitable point the institution and the individual can then come together to formalize the beginning of the tenure climb.

As reasonable as this practice sounds, it does not represent sound academic management. The American Association of University Professors in particular is opposed to it, for it obviously undercuts and cancels out the whole purpose of the six-year trial period. If the individual is granted an indefinite number of years to prove eligibility for permanent tenure, there is no point in maintaining the fiction of a trial period.

The practice also has an unwelcome impact on the academic marketplace, especially in a period of high unemployment. If the individuals are accorded indefinite years of probation and, in effect, given their own option as to when to get on the tenure ladder, they occupy positions that other persons farther along in their training want to be hired for. For the maximum welfare of the academic industry, it is obviously imperative to maintain an open traffic in job placements and terminations at the nontenure level. This means that vacancies should be declared promptly whenever an institution feels it can replace a dilatory hanger-on with a person possessing more training and greater drive. The six-year rule helps institutions do this, thus facilitating the always unpleasant job of weeding out the incompetent before it is too late. The rule serves to keep the pressure on the individual and thus to assist the institution in tagging the unpromising long before the traumatic up-or-out point is reached.

During the seventies and into the eighties, the courts have increasingly supported the A.A.U.P. on this point, holding, in effect, that a 100 percent contract, at no matter what rank or title, is a fulltime commitment and must therefore be counted as a probationary year. Hence, if an institution grants an individual six consecutive contracts at the rank of lecturer, for example, the institution signifies thereby that it considers these years to be probationary. It is therefore obligated to conduct the mandatory sixth-year review. The decision to be made is not up-or-out but rather tenure-or-out. If the institution fails to formalize its decision and proceeds to offer the individual a seventh contract, it has by that very action granted tenure, and the individual is home free. In the niceties of academic legalism, therefore, it is the 100-percentness of the contract rather than its rank, title, or tenure-symbol designation that matters.

A certain wry irony surrounds the concept of tenure itself as presently practiced in American higher education. Originally it was designed as a protective device for the innovative scholar and creative thinker. Academic freedom is vital to a free society and it means, among other things, the right to speak out on unpopular causes or to advance unorthodox and unconventional ideas. To protect that right, universities promised continuing employment to those who had proven themselves in the academic professions. At the present time, however, one rarely hears of anyone's job being threatened by what he or she believes or utters publicly. Instead, tenure is now thought of in economic terms; it is principally a device to protect job security. The lawsuits nowadays center not on a professor's right to say what he pleases but rather on his right to a job. Tenure began as a protection for the strong—the inventive, creative, and imaginatively offbeat. Now, in the strange inversions of contemporary life, it has been turned into a protection for the weak—the plodding, unresourceful drone who would find it difficult to get rehired in the open academic market.

Job security has overtaken not only the tenure concept; it now seems also to apply increasingly to the nontenured as well. In most universities it is extremely difficult to terminate an individual even during the six nontenured years. From a middle manager's viewpoint, the primary attention must now be focused on the original appointment. If mistakes are made there, a dean will require rigorous procedures, reams of paper, and a careful lawyer at the right hand to guide an unwanted professor out of the institution into another line of work.

From a management standpoint the ratio of tenured to nontenured professors represents an ongoing concern. On the one hand, any institution would wish to tenure any person of promise so as to strengthen the entire faculty. It is hard to let go of genuine competence, wherever it may be found. But if, over the years, there are too many of these, the faculty becomes "tenured in," making it difficult for the institution to change directions in its hiring patterns to respond to new program demands made by students. A ratio of 50:50 is generally thought to be optimum; if it reaches much above 70 percent tenured to 30 percent nontenured, an institution is in for trouble.

Another problem looms. With the decline in academic hiring and the accent increasingly placed on job security, many universities will see the tenure-to-nontenure ratio go up, regardless of the policies they follow. Professors get older. With each passing year, their salaries grow higher. In a stagnant, labor-intensive industry like higher education, many universities will find themselves not only tenured-in but also aged-in and dollared-in. The eighties and nineties are destined to be difficult decades for academic management.

Although the tenure concept and overattention to job security can retard a university's struggles toward excellence, there is something to be said for the superprotection most universities provide their employees. Aside from its human-

65

itarianism, it provides a stability and continuity to university life that can be argued for quite independent of its immediate psychological benefits. Intellectual work cannot flourish in an environment of abrupt changes and sudden shifts of direction. Neither can it flourish where there is an abundance of worries and insecurities in the polity of the organization. The snail's-pace deliberateness of university decision-making offers a steadiness of stimuli that lessens the need for quick response and coordinately enhances the opportunity for thoughtful reflection. This thoughtful reflection is what the best universities are made of.

# FIVE

# Outreach: The University as Urban Service Station

WHAT IS an "urban mission"? is one of those cliché questions that have clattered down the hallways of American higher education during the sixties and seventies earnestly and somewhat wistfully searching for an answer.

American educators have always carried themselves with a certain air of bravado when it comes to serving the people; and when some new demand is placed on them, like educating all American youth or providing general education for a free society, they are quick to adapt their craft or at least its rhetoric to the new political fashion. Like the general public, professional educators still nurse the myth that education is the final solution to society's ailments, so there is a characteristic boldness in their pronouncements about how education is to approach any new task.

But this business of urban mission, unlike earlier calls for response and adaptation, has caught the social activists off guard with their bravado uncovered, for this phrase, in one stroke, appears to be changing the assumptions about education's diagnostic and remedial powers. The urban mission cliché, for the first time, announces that there is such a thing as a distinctively *urban*, in contrast to *suburban* or *rural*, education. Here is a distinction we have not heard before. We are unfamiliar with the semantic tools necessary to deal with it.

Those who are historically minded are fond of pointing out that the Athenian academies and the medieval universities of Paris and Bologna were all urban institutions. Indeed, most of America's leading universities—Harvard, Berkeley, Stanford, Penn, Columbia, Chicago—were established and have flourished in a metropolitan environment. But that, of course, is not the point, since these schools have typically served a national and international clientele and have not thought of themselves as belonging to the parochial ambiance of their host cities.

To be urban, therefore, is more than just being physically situated inside the city limits. It has something to do with an institutional state of mind, a posture of response to some new, unfamiliar constituency. The nature of cities has changed. What used to be the quiet subservience of the citizenry has erupted into angry, militant, and highly volatile activism by a wide variety of political groups. The very fabric of the polity, the texture of citizenship itself, is under enormous strain in our major cities. And as it happens, the demand for higher education is one of those available issues around which shrill, belligerent discussion often develops.

The real question, therefore, both pointed and resistant to solution, is whether there is an explicitly urban orientation to higher education. To put the question more bluntly, what is urban about urban education?

It is an understatement to say that yards and yards of rhetoric have been spun out over this seemingly substantive question. It turns out, however, that a "quickie," short-form version of the answer can be found lying unnoticed in the underbrush of big-city politics and can be stated quite simply. Urban education is the education of racial and ethnic minorities. This means that if a university claims to be urban, it must be prepared to demonstrate that, whatever else it does, it is engaged actively in the recruitment, support, tutor-

68

ing, remediation, preparation, and eventual graduation of blacks, Chicanos, Puerto Ricans, and American Indians—the last group having now adopted a new designation that carries a not-so-subtle sociopolitical message, native Americans.

Of course, there are other things that may also belong under the rubric of urban education. Customarily, these are voiced in very general terms and are subsumed under the familiar phrase *addressing urban problems*. The natural scientists are expected to direct their investigations at pollution, transportation, and health delivery systems. The social scientists examine housing, commerce, and city planning. The humanists inquire into the value dynamics of living in an environment of human crowding, information overload, and the overpowering excess of sensory stimuli. But it is plain that making the urban-mission argument on the strength of these enterprises is not politically sufficient. There must be an overt, demonstrable commitment to the training and preparation of those who have for so many decades been frozen out of higher learning in America, namely, the economic underclasses and the racial and ethnic minorities now making their homes in the nation's cities.

There is no question that this focus has been central to new urban institutions recently under development. But this concept is, as noted, only the short-form version of the answer. If we were to examine more thoughtfully the total reach of the urban commitment, what would an unexpurgated definition of urban education turn out to be?

The idea that a university should be of direct service to the surrounding populace is a uniquely American notion. It all began with the Morrill Act, which President Lincoln signed in 1862. This milestone piece of legislation provided for grants of federal land to the several states, which were instructed to use proceeds from the sale or use of those lands to create institutions prepared to offer instruction in "agriculture and the mechanic arts." As we all know, these A and M colleges turned out to be an extremely popular political idea, and many of them have grown into so-called land-grant institutions of the first rank among American public and private universities.

Their original idea, however, is still referred to as the land-grant concept, and it is this concept that is usually summoned forth when the question of the urban mission is taken under study. For if the agricultural schools have been so spectacularly successful in serving the rural areas of America, a natural expectation follows that some analogous service can be delivered to urban citizens. Much of recent literature in higher education has been devoted to the careful construction of this analogy. However, it turns out to be a tricky enterprise, and we have come to much grief in spelling out the nature of an urban institution's clientele and how that clientele, if definable, can be serviced.

One of the problems of analogy building is to make sure the terms one is working with are genuinely equivalent. In the pairing of urban and rural social phenomena, this equivalence sometimes has to be forced. For example, the nineteenth-century agrarian economy of the United States was expansionist and exploratory in character. Within this context there developed a need for biological and botanical experimentation and an ancillary need to get the results of such investigations directly into the hands of those working the land. The society itself provided no ready agencies for this kind of work. It was therefore politically evident that a new kind of institution, an agricultural experiment station connected with a college of agriculture, should be deliberately created for this purpose. This development made a lot of sense to nineteenth-century politicians, and we all know the remarkable achievements that have followed from it.

In today's world, there is no question that many urban problems need studying, but it is not simultaneously true to say that no agencies exist for their study. Government agencies today have their own research arms for investigations into pollution, housing, and transportation. The private sector maintains its own research laboratories for the improvement of manufacturing processes, communication, and the invention of new products and techniques. In a very real sense, research and development themselves have been institutionalized in American life. They have been made a regular part of the entire structure of our socioeconomics, and in the process of institutionalization they have wound up outside higher education. Thus, the university as an investigative research center has arrived late. Or, better, it was never systematically consulted in earlier days when urban problems were beginning to reveal themselves in the management of city life. Whereas the farmer was trained to turn to the nearby agricultural school for answers, the city dweller did not similarly turn to the neighboring university for his. Thus, urban higher education in America has never developed a service interest, let alone a scholarly academic interest, in the kinds of inquiries that city life generates.

Another slippage in the analogy concerns the disparate focus of rural versus urban problems. The land-grant concept originally referred to questions of agronomy, crop rotation, development of hybrids, and farm resource management. All these are impersonal objects of inquiry, the kinds of things that a college of agriculture was set up to study. They are of the order of the physical sciences, pointing to phenomena out there in nature waiting to be understood by farmers for the furtherance of a better economy and, incidentally, for the turning of a better profit. Urban problems, on the other hand, are problems of people: education, jobs, crime, welfare, discrimination, zoning ordinances. These are the stuff of the social and behavioral sciences. They occupy the nonprofit side of social life. Furthermore, social sciences can never match the natural sciences for definitive solutions. Human beings, so much more complex than cows, soil, and kernels of corn, resist neat analysis and rigorous inquiry. Their behavior can be examined and plotted, but it cannot be *predicted* and *controlled*, two words dear to all scientists.

This means that the study of human problems is of a different order and is, inevitably, essentially a political activity. This, in turn, means that for an institution to claim to be urban, it must be political. It goes without saying that the higher education community chafes at this appalling prospect. University professors resent the intrusion of political considerations into academic decisionmaking. They see in this development a threat to academic freedom and a compromise of disinterested scholarship.

Nevertheless, in the hard realities of the new metropolis, the rules of the "town-gown" nexus have been changed. Whether they like it or not, urban faculties now are subject to a new element of control, the political impact of what they teach, how they teach, whom they admit to their classrooms, the academic standards they attempt to maintain, even the kinds of questions they choose to investigate and research, not to mention the conclusions they reach. The urban university, once the champion of open and objective inquiry, fearless of criticism and dogged about getting at the truth, is now the cautious entrepreneur of whatever the surrounding neighborhoods and subcultures demand or are willing to tolerate.

During the seventies, the middle manager more often than not became the broker of this new accommodation. With a traditional faculty on one side and a spirited, militant populace on the other, a dean's office became the interchange for the developing crossfire. Three examples may help to illustrate this phenomenon.

(1) A faculty committee draws up plans to recruit black students to prepare them as teachers for inner-city schools. The dean disseminates the report not only to other faculty but to teachers and administrators in the target schools for their study and reaction. Without the authorization of the dean, the proposal is reprinted and distributed to students within the university and lay groups within the surrounding neighborhoods. A delegation of students appears unannounced, forces its way into the dean's office, and amid shouts of obscenities demands that they, with their superior "street" wisdom, be empowered to design the courses for the projected program.

(2) Over the course of several months, a faculty curriculum

committee develops a comprehensive, interdepartmental master's degree program designed to upgrade social workers in Spanish-speaking neighborhoods. Copies of the proposal document find their way into neighborhood citizens' organizations. When the dean calls a faculty meeting for final ratification of the proposal, a group of Chicano citizens, together with faculty sympathizers, physically disrupts the meeting, denouncing the proposal as racist and demanding its defeat. The meeting turns into a verbal brawl between neighborhood residents and faculty members, and the dean is forced to declare an adjournment with action postponed indefinitely.

(3) A Puerto Rican professor comes up for promotion to associate professor. Her dossier is exhaustively prepared and copies of it are distributed to the tenured professors on the promotion committee. At a meeting of this committee called and conducted by the dean, one of the candidate's colleagues unilaterally and without authorization invites into the meeting room a delegation of professors from other colleges on the campus demanding her promotion. They shout down the remarks of the other members of the committee and hurl abuse at the dean for not pushing enthusiastically for favorable action.

In these confrontations of the early seventies, the language was angry, the tone ugly, and the hostility toward the university bitter and unrelenting. In these encounters, the dean was the quintessential flak-catcher, taking both institutional and personal abuse. Yet he or she was expected to turn aside the most acrimonious and vile assaults with calm, reasoned explanations of how the university operates and how academic decisions are made. Such explanations, however, inflamed the protesters even more; for it was the very procedures of the university, the hated "system," that was the focus of their outrage. These procedures, these racist rules, regulations, and standards, they alleged, had been keeping minority persons out of the white man's university! And the ranting, virulent attack resumed.

Although difficult to appreciate in the heat of these sessions, there was a considerable amount of play-acting on the part of both sides. The protesters had a legitimate point to make, i.e., that the American university had seemed exclusionary in racial and ethnic makeup, if not by witting policy then by the inadvertent effect of the traditional modes of admission and employment. But the protesters knew that the people who run our universities are, for the most part, white, guilt-burdened liberals. Playing the right stops on this guilt, therefore, was the place to begin. It was the softening-up phase, the prologue to the revolutionary soap opera to follow. It is important, then, to see that these confrontations were never staged on the rational level, but rather at the emotional, choleric level.

It is easy to intimidate a white liberal if you go directly for the jugular and call him a racist. The mau-mauing of a dean, thus, was turned into a stage production. It was deliberately escalated to the inflammatory level so as to puncture the dean's institutional *persona*, that mode of organizational style and behavior characterized earlier as *coolth* and seen as a necessary element for institutional stability. In this histrionic way, the protesters attacked the character, not the intelligence, of the manager. It was designed to make him crack, lose his temper, and lash out with inflammatory remarks in response.

For his or her part, the dean read the script prepared for the managerial staff. First, one tried to quiet the protesters, suggesting that a delegation of two or three represent them in more subdued talks. Of course, the protesters did not want that, since that would force the discussion back toward the rational level. This failing, the dean then proceeded to answer all questions as quietly and sanely as possible, with the eventual object of outlasting the violent improvisational theater in progress and easing the militants out of the room.

Sometimes a promise to consider the problem was enough, but both sides knew that this was merely a pro forma gambit. Some concrete step was required, perhaps the appointment of a special faculty comittee to look into the matter. But before this option was formalized, the dean's script called for a condition, namely, that the protesters put their protest in writing before the special committee convened. Customarily, any self-respecting protester would have balked at this requirement since it tended to force the dialogue back toward the rational level. Furthermore, revolutionary rhetoric doesn't sound half so scary on paper. It must be shouted with angry visage for maximum effect.

It so happens, however, that the middle manager, like faculty colleagues throughout the establishment, is preeminently print-oriented. If the protest had substance, the protesters would have done well to accept the invitation. In a university setting, print is politically the most potent medium. As Marshall McLuhan told us many years ago, the linear, task-oriented mind of the academic administrator works best from the written word. A university officer can eventually work free of confrontations of oral bombast, but a written document must be answered. Its message, no matter how trivial, gets caught up in the communication apparatus of the organization. Many eyes must examine its contents. Advisory memos must be prepared on the proper course of response. A written document enjoys far greater status in a university office than does a moving, emotional appeal for justice delivered orally in a crowded hall. Hence, the more intelligent protesters have always known that genuine remedial action—if that is what they really wanted—was achievable through written manifestos and memorandums rather than through stormy, face-to-face meetings.

For the middle manager in a political encounter, it was well to remember the militants' iron law of protest: always escalate your demands! The militants' typical game plan was to crank up their confrontations in order to find a crack in the institutional armor. Any concession, no matter how seemingly slight or insignificant, provoked an even louder, more incendiary blast of rhetoric, and the list of grievances was certain to lengthen. The wisest as well as saddest of deans learned that attempting to mollify the militants through thoughtful accommodation often turned out to be the most destructive course of action.

What then is the political lesson we learned from these encounters so typical of our campuses during the sixties and seventies? The answer lies beyond rhetoric, beyond the play-acting, beyond the script. It has something to do with holding on to *university values*. As romantic and amorphous as that phrase may sound, it stands for a network of standards and expectations intrinsic to the vitality and integrity of the academic world. Central to them all is the principle of reason. And reason has gone into the formulation of a university's statutes, its policies, its procedures for settling disputes. For all their seeming obtuseness, a university's governing by-laws and practices do have a rational base.

In crisis management, therefore, when the air is heavy with tension and the language is vile and insulting, the safest and at the same time most constructive course is to repair to the university's conventional way of doing business. In the face of overt attack, the dean's most promising strategy is to be faithful to the university's rules and to the procedures by which these rules are changed. In the end, it is to be faithful to the faculty who, for the most part, are responsible for promulgating those rules and are the ones responsible for their periodic reexamination. If the rules and standards seem to have a racist effect, if they appear to discriminate against one class but not against another, if they foment disharmony unnecessarily, then they may be in need of overhaul. In most universities, the procedures for overhaul are already in place. Admissions requirements are modified through regular channels. The criteria for faculty promotion and tenure are subject always to the systematic scrutiny of members of the community through well understood pathways of review. Finally, university statutes provide regularized procedures for their own amendment.

\* \* \*

In the larger perspective provided by hindsight, we may now be in a position to learn still other lessons about university management in a changing, urban America. For one thing, the counterculture has played a trick on ethnic minorities in this country over the past decade. During the rising expectations of the sixties and seventies, the blacks and Latins were launching a powerful attack on the nation's institutions, demanding to be let in, to be included, to be allowed to share in the social and psychological goods provided by those institutions. As we have seen, one of the most successful salients of that offensive was directed at the nation's colleges and universities. Among the minorities' staunchest allies in this endeavor were the affluent children of white America, many of them using the country's campuses as loitering stations to avoid service in the armed forces or entry into responsible adulthood. They encouraged the notion that college is the middle-class's gateway to money and power and that until it is made available to minorities in much greater numbers, it is a racist sector of American society. They demanded that their brothers and sisters be allowed to join them.

But in the late seventies and into the eighties, just about the time that blacks and Latins had made a dent in the academic consciousness and pried open some doors, the counterculture supporters turned to a new theme, i.e., the pointlessness of a college education. Far from being the middle-class ticket to money, power, and influence, they now argued, it was instead a monumental waste of time. What the ethnic minorities had just won at such cost in time, effort, and emotional drain was now discredited before their eyes and made to appear worthless and futile. Even worse, higher education was advertised as a mind depressant, a killer of natural man. Thus did another minor pendulum in the intricate clockwork of society make a full, divisive swing.

As would be expected, the minorities showed themselves to be unaffected by this defection from their movement for greater access to higher education. Increasingly, they ignored the claim that university training was meaningless and, instead, began to turn their early victories into beachheads of influence in their institutions. The irony is that in the heady enthusiasm of their new power, they found themselves once again in danger of being sidetracked into blind alleys, this time by responsible university officials.

The urban university's commitment to its clientele remains what it has always been, namely, to provide a place where the student may develop the skills and understandings he or she must acquire to succeed in mainstream culture. But, in pressing their early demands, the minority groups seemed too eager to settle for too little. Instead of asking to be allowed in as full members of a student body, to study the full gamut of programs and offerings, they asked for programs merely about themselves, and university officials were all too accommodating in allowing them this self-defeating option. First came black studies, a pressure-driven response to black militancy in the late sixties. Then came native American studies and Latin American studies in the early seventies. In the mid-seventies, we saw the emergence of Slavic studies for urban Poles, and bilingual-bicultural education as a resurgence of the Latin demand, with feminist studies running alongside the bandwagon trying somehow to get on board.

The question is whether these new programs represent genuine disciplines or whether they are the university's subtle sop to political power groups. During the sixties and seventies, the nation's colleges and universities have shown themselves to be easily intimidated, and as a result they have continued tinkering with their curriculums out of some political desire to be well thought of on the editorial page. But the truth is that the demands of the mainstream culture for brains and talent are not likely to change. Whether or not these programs are or are not genuine disciplines is therefore beside the point. The central question is whether they lead anywhere in today's world. Increasingly the answer to that question seems to be no.

From a purely institutional point of view, the middle manager must recognize that the ultimate racism is to concoct programmatic deadends. Creation of the above programs may have temporarily quieted the militants, but the long-run effect of these curricular diversions can only be to retard the educational progress of the minority student, to slow down his or her entry into full participation in the American system. If the yield of a college education were only to make it easier for the ethnic to rap with his neighbors, these programs might be appropriate. But if the ethnic wants to get a job downtown and eventually pursue a career, he must prepare himself in the skills the downtown establishments continue to want.

Increasingly, minority students are waking up to this truth. They are turning away from these special studies programs, opting to reenter the established academic and professional majors. As they do so, however, they run into the opposite problem—that is, the old-line majors, many of them grounded in the liberal arts, have not changed in forty years. When it comes to urban relevance, they have been, and still are, "out of it." The sixties and seventies have swept past them, leaving no whiff of changing air, no fresh insights into the meaning of the traditional subjects of academe for youth of the eighties. The typical arts and sciences faculty is a contradiction: they are more liberal than their colleagues when viewing the outside world, and more conservative than Warren G. Harding when viewing themselves and their curriculum. Their usual response to criticism of their traditionalism is that they are teaching "the unchanging values of the West" and, by doing so, "speaking to the ages." But we all know that nowadays, there is just so much mileage in this argument. A dean in a liberal arts setting, especially in an urban environment, must engineer a more open, yes, more *liberal* attitude among his colleagues toward the idea of curricular change. Given such modernization, the genuinely liberal arts, in vital linkage with professional programs in engineering, business, medicine, education, journalism, architecture, law, social work, and the other disciplines, can once again be recognized as the working ticket to the wider community.

If the urban university must be political, therefore, its politics must be broader and more sophisticated. Instead of responding, one at a time, to this or that power-pressure group, the urban university must engage its Land-Grant mentality with the whole community, recognizing that the energy of city life is not confined to ethnic neighborhoods and barrios but is metropolitan in scope and outlook. The university is, after centuries of refinement, still a *uni*versity, a place where people come together to share the rich deposit of their civilization and to develop some common outlook, some unifying orientation to their world.

* * *

Having said this, however, one larger question remains. The genius of the American experiment is its enjoyment and active use of diversity. What then is the university's role in developing the *E pluribus* side of our national motto? Our great cities are where the plurality of our society is so rich, so intense, so politically magnified. To deliver on the urban mission promise within a land-grant context then is bound to be mixed up somehow with the wealthy variation among our people, not just in language or culture, but in the meaning they attach to life.

The philosophers have a word for it, *phenomenology*. Each of us grows up inside a set of givens: sex, time, place, parents, neighborhood, social class. In our interaction with these constants, we develop a personal history out of which we shape our notions of ourselves and those around us. We come to define our situation—our work, our living space, our values, our loves—in terms of what it expects of us and what we expect of it. These expectations themselves move, grow, and often grind against the expectations of others. We all know the primary points of abrasion: class, color, language, sex, and age. In city life today, individual phenomenologies are in collision! This, one might say, is the essence of the urban condition.

Most of us are distressed and demoralized by this state of things. We feel the hard edge of hate and distrust against ourselves. And we find disturbingly greater traces of these poisons in our own feelings toward others as the environment around us becomes more violent and hostile. Is there a way out, a way back, a way up to a new condition of respect and trust among our fellow citizens?

Every institution in the American culture will have to define its own contribution, if any, to this difficult passage. For the university's part, the task will not be easy, but there is a sense in which a university might turn out to be the central player in this enterprise. A university, after all, is specifically designed for the accommodation of differences. It is a place where arguments are not only expected but encouraged. Out of the clash of ideas, we have always been told, comes truth. Why not then turn the university into an arena for the clash of phenomenologies? Can the university serve as a forum for these encounters as it has so nobly and successfully served for five centuries as a forum in the purely intellectual realm?

Chapter 3 reported on an unsuccessful experiment in this area, the ill-fated brown-bag forum. In that case the vaunted objectivity of the academic person buckled. In this confrontation between contending phenomenologies, the intellectual's time-honored stance of disinterested analysis seemed to break apart, yielding to commonplace fear and animus.

But perhaps this is just the point. Getting one's consciousness raised is painful. And yet, once experienced, it leads to a fuller, more sophisticated witness to other people's lives. It engenders a more generous appreciation of what others think, feel, and want. In the end, it illuminates the self and brings to awareness features of one's makeup which were previously unrecognized. What more appropriate undertaking by the modern university than to provide for the enhancement of self-understanding?

Looking closely, we can discern in the hallways and seminar rooms of the urban university of the eighties a readiness for this kind of effort. Now that the belligerent confrontations of the last decades have subsided in frequency and intensity, we seem to have entered upon an epoch of more subdued consideration of social diversity. In the language of the age, we call it cultural pluralism. The urban university is in the right spot at the right time to take hold of this concept and lift discourse to a new level. As things have turned out, the examination of pluralism is the one new element in American higher education; and the urban institution, because of its location, its clientele, and its land-grant heritage, has been selected as the sponsor and impresario of this new venture.

What makes urban education urban? This question raised earlier received a tentative, short-form answer. But a more considered, sophisticated answer might be something like this: not the pandering to this or that political group but the thoughtful, open exploration of phenomenological diversity among us and how our mutual understanding of that diversity can become the occasion for a new unity among us.

There is no question that the task will be difficult. The conditions of the spirit on our campuses are fragile and uneasy. But the make-or-break issue for our urban institutions is at hand, and their delivery on this mission will soon tell us whether there is in fact an urban version of the land-grant concept.

# Affirmative Action: Equity and What It Means

THE PREVIOUS CHAPTER has examined the extramural, off-campus politics of minority protest and how it is translated into programs for students. Equally important are the in-house manifestations of the protest movement and the ways in which minorities—especially blacks and women—have pressed their case for equal opportunity within the faculty and administrative ranks.

Like most establishment institutions, higher education has traditionally been ruled by white males. Furthermore, since higher education operates its own "farm system," i.e., the network of graduate schools supplying new PhD's, the white-male ruling class has controlled entry to the academic profession itself and has monopolized decisionmaking as to who shall survive there. No wonder then that during the civil-rights upheavals of the late sixties and the consciousness-raising movements of the seventies, colleges and universities found themselves in a beleaguered, defensive position on the minorities issue.

The track record on the surface was not good. Blacks had always been underrepresented on our nation's campuses, and women had found their way into university work in significant numbers only in nursing, education, social work, home economics, and physical education. In these and other disciplines, they were frequently paid less than men, promoted more slowly than men, and consistently denied prestigious committee assignments and policymaking committee chairmanships. In the upper, most prestigious echelons of the professoriate—the research faculties—women and minorities are still conspicuous by their almost total absence. In the late seventies, a midwestern urban university convened an all-campus group of professors to oversee the establishment of research centers and institutes in that institution. The thirteen who attended were all white males.

In the all too familiar protocols of male chauvinism, women have wound up as notetakers, committee scribes, coffee jockeys and arrangers of academic social functions. Even into the eighties, their position on most campuses is still tentative and provisional. Most important, except for newsworthy exceptions, women are almost totally missing from administrative leadership positions in the nation's colleges and universities.

University faculties and administrative staffs, for all their white maleness, like to think of themselves as enlightened and compassionate, readier than other sectors of society to respond to the pleas of the oppressed and downtrodden. The truth is, however, that higher education is one of the most conservative institutions in America. Contrary to their counterculture utterances and their continuing identification with the Democratic party, university faculties do not like change, either inside their academic enclaves or in the social order as a whole.

For example, when national movements of consciousness-raising began in earnest in the 1960s, individual faculty members wrote letters to the editor in support of greater minority employment. But these same individuals did not translate this new awareness to their own circumstances, and accordingly saw no reason to change the hiring practices or promotion policies that had served them so well for so long.

When it came to identifying new faculty members, it was business as usual. The so-called "Old Boy" network worked fine!

The iceberglike stolidity of university personnel practices did not go long unnoticed in the corridors of the federal government. Executive Order 11246, signed by President Lyndon B. Johnson on September 24, 1965 (subsequently amended by Executive Order 11375) had this to say:

> . . . all Government contracting agencies shall include in every Government contract hereafter entered into the following provisions:
>
> "During the performance of this contract, the contractor agrees as follows:
>
> "(1) The contractor will not discriminate against any employee or applicant for employment because of race, color, religion, sex, or national origin. The contractor will take affirmative action to ensure that applicants are employed, and that employees are treated during employment, without regard to their race, color, religion, sex, or national origin."

In its original conception this landmark order was aimed at defense contractors and other firms doing regular business with the federal government. But since federal grants to colleges and universities could technically be construed as transforming these institutions into contracting agencies, it was not long before the Department of Health, Education, and Welfare and the Equal Employment Opportunity Commission discovered a whole new world of enforcement opening up before them. Accordingly, they moved quickly in the late sixties to require institutions receiving federal funds to demonstrate—through explicit, overt initiatives—that they were providing fairness and equal opportunity to both prospective and continuing employees.

The original directives coming out of Washington were understandably hesitant and exploratory. But during the late sixties, as federal civil-rights bureaucrats became more sophisticated in their promulgation of rules and guidelines, they also became more aggressive. They began to push for compensatory actions, i.e., making up for past injustices by overhiring of minority group members. Their pronouncements began to carry explicit mention of quotas of positions to which minority members were entitled and to goals of racial and sexual balance within departments. Understandably, these implied requirements created a stir on many campuses. The concept of quotas had always been considered nefarious and repugnant. In an earlier day, for a college admissions office to limit Jewish enrollment by some arbitrary percentage figure exemplified an outrageous affront to the merit principle. And yet now, in the sixties and seventies, the principle of quotas was being advanced, not casually but as a matter of governmental policy, by federal agencies eager to show results on the "affirmative action" front.

Institutional resistance to quotas and goals produced an expected result. Federal enforcement officers sensed that the higher education community was hiding behind some abstract moral principle to avoid hiring blacks and women. The universities bridled at this charge, claiming that racial and sexual imbalance was traceable to the fact that the pool of candidates from which they customarily drew their new faculty was itself severely out of balance. Each year's crop of new PhD's was mostly white and male, like the crops before. How could an institution be expected to establish a quota of, say, 50 percent females in department X if the annual crop of PhD's in X was only 10 percent female? To the universities, this seemed a legitimate response, but its obvious effect was to prompt the chase after a new quarry, the graduate schools. Federal affirmative action officers were grateful for having their villains pointed out and they took off after them.

As for the hiring process itself, the clear and present target was the "Old-Boy" network. Acknowledging that their own hiring pools were possibly too restrictive, institutions acquiesced in a new requirement that all openings must be publicly advertised. Earlier this practice had been considered somewhat uncivilized, permitted only anonymously in the back pages of the *Bulletin of the American Association of University Professors*. Now, however, explicit ads were to be placed in the *Chronicle of Higher Education*, the *New York Times*, the institution's local major newspapers, and selected journals covering the specialty being sought.[1]

Even some minor newspapers got into the act. In the late seventies, the leading black newspaper in a large midwestern city noticed sharply increased traffic in requests for such ads. The explanation was that their neighboring institutions, to satisfy affirmative action auditors, were routinely including such public notice for each opening in their advertising budgets. Sensing the possibilities of this, the newspaper began monitoring vacancies in all metropolitan institutions. If a help-wanted ad for a given vacancy was not forthcoming, the newspaper would file a discrimination grievance with the local office of H.E.W.

The yield from ads in all outlets has indeed expanded the pool! Universities now receive veritable haystacks of applications, sometimes hundreds of vitas and resumes for a single position. The task of winnowing these piles of paper to find the few who are genuinely qualified continues to require enormous numbers of faculty and staff hours. University officers report that the end result of this mass-broadcast method does not differ substantially from what a more selective approach produces—except for one major change: academic advertising is now a major budget item, draining precious funds away from the educational program of most institutions.

The public advertising strategy, like so many other government intrusions, has produced an ironic backlash. It has become so inefficient in time and money, albeit virtually man-

---

[1] *The Chronicle of Higher Education*, in particular, has enjoyed the windfall from this requirement. Founded in the early sixties as a type of monthly newsletter, the *Chronicle* enters the eighties as a major house organ for academia, expanded in size and converted to biweekly status. The publication now rakes in hundreds of thousands of advertising dollars annually and sometimes devotes over half its pages to academic placement notices.

datory, that many university officers have reverted to the trusty Old-Boy network to identify minority candidates. This network is not without its virtues. In an age when confidential references are no longer possible, the statements one reads in an applicant's placement dossier have to be discounted as worthless. The personal telephone call is still the most accurate information channel.

The public advertising contrivance has been reduced to a pro forma nuisance, a token ticket to compliance that no one except equal-employment-opportunity officers takes seriously. Nevertheless, affirmative action has become big business on most campuses, especially in the public sector of higher education, which is expected to be more politically vigilant on the minority question. But big business brings with it big bureaucracy. Every procedure of the search-and-hiring process must now be carefully monitored. The precise rhetoric of the job description, the careful phrasing of the newspaper advertisement, the preliminary screening of candidates' dossiers, the interviewing of the finalists, and the documentation of reasons supporting the selection of the ultimate winner—all these steps require elaborate forms to be filled out, checked over, approved by layers of administrators, and finally filed away in the archives to provide the "paper trail" that must be exhibited to the visiting federal auditor on demand. It is a slow and costly business that drains huge sums in the institutional budget from the gut work of the university—teaching and research.

Affirmative action has also produced another unhealthy side-effect on some campuses by engendering a kind of in-house paranoia leading to an unnamed form of institutional masochism. It is understandable that federal compliance officers are always on watch, like Big Brother, to see if good faith is operating. But within the institution, even before any fact-finding operations have been initiated, there has sometimes developed a debilitating assumption, namely, that the institution is guilty! In those places where corrective actions have been taken quietly many years ago, such an attitude, if

88

permitted to flourish unchecked, can breed corrosive distrust and bitterness among otherwise amiable and cooperative colleagues. Worst of all, it leads to injudicious decisions with disastrous fallout that can be fully appreciated only months or years later.

For example, in a rush to redress the imbalance of races and sexes in faculty positions, some institutions have reluctantly appointed minority persons to positions the hiring institution knew in advance they could not handle. This set in motion a course of events that can only end in heartbreak and recrimination, for it is obviously much more difficult to remove a minority person from his or her position than a white male. Indeed, any criticism whatsoever can quickly be taken as overt racism or sexism and can be carried as a formal complaint to a higher officer. In these days of instantaneous reflex to imagined insult, it is virtually impossible for a white-male middle manager to defend himself against such attacks. The complainant is always presumed right in claiming to have been wronged!

Another tendency born of rash and hasty affirmative actions was the overpromotion of minority group members, pushing them up in the hierarchy of the organization for token show purposes before they had established a track record of performance as was expected of everybody else. This special form of condescending racism says subtly but loudly: "You can't make it by the usual standards. Don't worry, I'll see to it that you get promoted to associate professor anyway, so that we can keep our minority percentage up to the required level!" It is hard to imagine any more destructive personnel policy—patronizing to the presumed beneficiary and seen as arbitrary favoritism by the remainder of the organization.[2]

As we turn into the eighties, university officers have begun to learn how to defend themselves against the countervailing

[2] For a bitter illustration, see Matthew Davidson, "Affirmative Action's Second Generation: In the Matter of Vilma Hernandez," *Change Magazine* 11 (November–December 1979):42–46.

influences of federal affirmative action inanities. One favorite method is to outbureaucratize the feds! When a federal agency requests information on hiring procedures and practices, the response deliberately takes on the clutter and clumsiness of a huge organization, one in which many right hands and many left hands do not know what the others are doing. By trying to simulate the federal government, clever university functionaries can unload mountains of data, most of it indigestible, on the not altogether unsuspecting federal agency. What follows is a slow, cumbersome exchange of communications, memoranda, information-seeking interrogatories, feasibility reports, task-force analyses, comparative equity studies, and obfuscatory interpretations in both directions. The university usually loses, but at least the timetable has been slowed down and the damage to the institution kept to a minimum. University administrators enter these paper-shuffling tournaments necessarily at a disadvantage. Not only are they presumed guilty at the outset, but their primary attention is elsewhere, on the educational program. For the feds, on the other hand, this is their job, their career. Their focus is on compliance—compliance on their terms. Never having worked in a university, they are ignorant of its goals, its special circumstances, and the derivative protocols and conventions that enable it to function. They always win, if not out of bureaucratic patience, because in the end the power—the Department of Justice—is on their side.

\*   \*   \*

As the above indicates, equity considerations enjoy high visibility at appointment time and in promotion decisions. They surface also in the lesser channels of managerial decisionmaking: the assignment of workload, the allocation of research money, the allotment of square footage of office space, and access to other sundry goodies of professoring such as travel money, secretarial assistance, and parking space.

However, the one area toward which all affirmative action

passions gravitate is salary. Salary is an area that has a special attraction for affirmative action activists. It is one of the few remaining aspects of academic life not governed by committee. Correspondingly, it is an area of managerial prerogative and is necessarily judgmental in character. Finally, although judgmental, it yields hard, comparable dollar figures whose meaning is unequivocal. For all of these reasons, the salary area is a made-to-order tournament ground for protest. It is where the heady vapors of "economic justice" intoxicate all those present.

As noted in chapter 4, the annual review of contributions in teaching, research, and service is intended to yield a recommendation from the dean to higher officers concerning the individual's salary level for the succeeding year. In the present chapter, salary setting is examined through a different lens, i.e., through a glass that magnifies the comparison of one faculty member with another.

In times past, the setting of salaries was a matter for the middle manager's private conscience. Moreover, the final determinations were always considered confidential, a kind of privileged communication between the academic executive and the individual professor. Today, however, in the freedom-of-information era, salaries are no more confidential than the annual outlay for typewriter ribbons or fuel oil. And since salaries represent the one most significant index by which individuals judge their own worth, it is little wonder that, whenever faculty salaries are published, they arouse primitive impulses in the body academic.

Although salary rewards for quality performance of an individual can be arrived at with some justification, the comparison of salaries, one with another, introduces a new set of considerations. The manager must now be able to demonstrate not only that a salary increase for A bears some rational relationship to A's performance but also that A's increase is fair vis-à-vis the increases for B, C, D, and, indeed, every other individual in the organization. Any change in a given salary obviously changes the relative position of every other. For this reason the question of salary equity is a judgment area calling for the prudent balancing of a large number of variables. It represents a far more complex thicket of decisionmaking than is generally recognized in management literature.

Of course, the equal-pay-for-equal-work principle does not have to be argued for. In universities, as elsewhere, it is expected that those with similar responsibilities will be assigned equivalent compensation. But in matters of salary equity, this is really not the issue. The critical determination is the overall value of the individual to the organization, a far more elusive, judgmental criterion than the mere equation between job assignments.

The phrase *overall value to the organization* brings to the surface what had hitherto been a part of the working subconscious of the middle manager. It had never been spelled out before, and professors as a rule did not dispute a dean's ultimate judgment. Nowadays, however, when an administrator's very thought processes are on trial, a dean is obligated to make overt and explicit what had earlier been private and intuitive. The phrase implies not only that an individual's value is a quality that can be identified and communicated to others, but also that it can be objectively quantified so as to lead to a specific dollar figure. Can this, in fact, be done? The answers vary. Some say that trying to quantify the comparison between professors is an apples and oranges predicament in a new setting. However, in this instance the stakes, if not higher, are tangled up with ego, status, and motivation—all touchy but vital elements of group morale and organizational vitality.

In approaching this task the middle manager must recognize a hard, ineluctable truth characteristic of all organizational life: every person considers himself underpaid. Hence, every salary decision by a dean is ipso facto inequitable. With this as a starting condition in all payroll analysis— and assuming the merit principle operating—what are the comparative variables a dean must introduce into the calculations before arriving at final salary figures? There are a number of them.

An original decision that produces equity problems later on is the dean's judgment concerning differential starting salaries. In chapter 4, attention was drawn to previous experience and training as two variables justifying higher-than-average initial pay levels. Now consider a hypothetical case of two prospective appointees. One individual may be a young, inexperienced PhD fresh out of graduate school. The other may be a PhD who has concluded five years of work testing the value of her doctoral training in the practical world and now has decided to enter academic work. For both individuals this is the first university position, and both are brought in at the assistant-professor level. If the experience record of the second individual is considered important to the hiring college, a salary add-on for this person would be in order.

In subsequent years, the annual reviews for these two individuals both indicate satisfactory performance. Should the experienced individual continue to have a salary advantage over the inexperienced one or should the salary differential between them be gradually closed? If the former option is taken, it would require the dean to grant higher pay increases to the inexperienced professor even though they are both performing satisfactorily.

An analogous hypothetical case concerns two individuals who join the faculty at the same level, but have been earning different salaries in their previous jobs. Individual A earned $14,000 last year and demands $15,000. Individual B earned $16,000 and demands $17,000. In every other respect the two are substantially equal in caliber, the institution wants both, and they are both hired at the requested figures. Is this equitable from a management point of view? And, as in the prior example, is the dean to allow the salary differential to persist year after year or is the higher paid individual to be given small increments and the lower paid individual large increments, even though the two of them are performing at a satisfactory level?

The answers to these questions are not to be found in any dean's manual. If the precise, quantifiable equivalence of two individuals could hypothetically be established, it might possibly be argued that their salaries likewise should be brought into correspondence. But no dean has ever claimed such powers of computerlike insight, and no set of faculty-originated guidelines could possibly produce such a finding. A dean's office is not a hypothetical place; rather it is a crossroads where real factors are weighed and final judgments are made. The production of judgments is what a dean is hired to do. If the salary differential was based upon sound reasoning in the first place, any later tampering with that differential undercuts the validity of the original judgment.

Other equity complications develop over seniority. Full Professor Smith has been in rank for ten years. She is now near the top of the salary range. Associate Professor Jones is promoted to Full Professor on the strength of a bibliography as long as Smith's, a national reputation equal to Smith's, and institutional contributions equivalent to Smith's. Should Professor Jones's salary in his first year in rank be set equal to that of Professor Smith in her tenth? No. Seniority is one of those unarguable artifacts of labor economics. A middle manager is bound to respect it in salary calculations. Throughout all levels of the American labor force, it has enjoyed a long, legitimate history as a wage criterion.

Finally, consider one of the most troublesome equity problems in university decisionmaking, namely, the "market value" of a professor. Professors R and S are both earning $20,000. Professor R is being wooed by another university with an offer of $25,000. She doesn't want to leave, but she takes her job offer letter to the dean and asks, "Can you match this?"

Traditional management theory stipulates that an employer should always pay a person the full measure of what that person is worth, so that when higher bids come in, the employer can avoid being put in a bargaining bind. In real life, however, what a person is worth is itself determined by what other people think. Hence, a demonstrable measure of one's institutional value is what somebody else is willing to pay.

In the above example, the dean ponders and with a counteroffer of $22,500 persuades Professor R to stay. Professor S is informed of this by grapevine or otherwise, and he forthwith demands the same salary. The dean turns him down. Is that a fair and equitable decision? Yes.

The market-value criterion has aroused ambivalent attitudes. Some institutions have explicitly disallowed it in equity disputes. That is to say, a dean may not justify one professor's salary being higher than another's on grounds of an accepted counteroffer. But in the interlinkage of administrative options, this policy would appear untenable, for if it were literally held to, it would mean that all equivalent professors at a given rank are entitled to the salary paid to the professor with the highest market value as measured by his or her outside offers. Moreover, it is commonplace to arrange for counteroffers so as to retain valuable and prestigious professors. Indeed, some institutions maintain a special fund for just this purpose. To institutionalize such increments and then rule them irrelevant in equity discussions is a contradiction in terms.

* * *

Affirmative action and, indeed, the entire concept of equity have been converted into political weapons. It all began, innocently enough, back in the sixties. In those exuberant days of a growth mentality and bountiful budgets, the demand for university jobs by blacks was understandably strong and vocal. Universities attempted to respond to this demand, but in doing so, they revealed an unexpected willingness to compromise their customary standards and yield to political pressure. Blacks were hired with credentials that would have been patently insufficient for any white applicant. The PhD degree, the traditional union card of the academic, was sometimes not required of minority candidates.

Blackness itself seemed to be the overpowering credential.

The federal government seemed to encourage the polit-icizing tendencies of affirmative-action thinking. During the late seventies, the Equal Employment Opportunity Commis-sion became increasingly blunt in its regulations. It came to refer to minority groups as *protected classes*, apparently sig-nifying that certain groups in our society needed special shielding from the predatory assaults of other groups. This phrase came as a surprise to many middle managers in col-leges and universities. It seemed to be announcing a new, virulent turn in affirmative-action affairs. The phrase was clearly out of keeping with the open, let-the-best-person-win protocols the universities were trying to live up to.

Affirmative action has also had another, more subtle but more debilitating, impact on academic human relations. The federal government's powers of intimidation against university administrators has clearly put most of them on the defensive. Given the antiadministrator syndrome on our nation's campuses, it is no surprise that faculty groups have taken advantage of the weakened position of academic management in this epoch of minority activism. Deans and vice-presidents have always been fair game for attacks from disgruntled faculty members. Now the warfare has esca-lated. The equity rhetoric has provided the faculty with new artillery.

\* \* \*

What has affirmative action brought? There is no question that the American university has been jolted out of its self-satisfied slumber on the discrimination question. In the typi-cal academic obsession with self-flagellation[3] and the equally typical proclivity for solving problems with endless commit-tees and elaborate bureaucratic superstructures, the Ameri-can professoriate has moved vigorously to establish the mechanisms for handling complaints and for watchdogging the affirmative-action trail. On most campuses the more fla-

[3] Someone has referred to university professors as "closet masochists."

grant abuses are on the way to being rectified. Hiring is, if not efficient, at least more open. Promotion committees are more assiduously color- and gender-blind. Salary lists are now made public so that everyone can get a crack at deciding what is equitable and what is not.

But, to hazard an understatement, the job is not over. So far the yield of affirmative-action activity is not spectacular. The American Council on Education reported early in the seventies that between 1969 and 1973, the percentage of blacks on college faculties rose from 2.1 to 2.9 and that of women from 19.1 to 20. Although similar figures have not been kept by the council, there is little evidence that the eighties can offer any more encouraging news. These inch-worm advances may indicate sluggish conditions in the PhD pipeline near the source of supply, i.e., the graduate schools, suggesting that it may be easier for a federal bureaucrat to tell a university whom to hire than a graduate school who should be awarded a PhD. As we learn more about academic careers and the motivations that advance them, we may discover that opening up the pipeline into and through our graduate schools is likely to be very long-term and discouragingly tedious. An analogy might be a symphony orchestra, also a dominantly white-male institution. Just as it requires at least twenty-five years to produce a performing musician, so likewise the preparation of a professor starts in childhood and covers a similar length of time, not merely a three-year stint in a graduate school.

Although the pipeline and the pool of candidates it yields is the long-run corrective, the pool that exists today must be more vigorously combed and searched. If genuinely qualified persons are out there, they must be brought into the hiring stream quickly and fairly. Also, what remain to be corrected on most campuses are the not-so-flagrant, subtle inequities that continue to dog the social environment. We need salary equity, but the language needs work too. If generic linguistic conventions in the masculine gender are offensive, we need more graceful substitutes for the mind-numbing locutions of *he or she* and *him or her*.

Affirmative action has without question raised the academic consciousness. But in its clumsy, insensitive, bureaucratic blundering it has produced countervailing excesses the academic community will spend decades paying for. Government sponsored "fairness" has come at a heavy price: a polarized academic community, widespread distrust of all decisionmakers, and a forced concern for one's own survival. As the eighties open, the once invigorating idea of colleagueship is seriously eroded, not likely to be restored for many years. There is a breakdown in the fabric of academic human relations. Like many other institutions, the university is losing a sense of personal and organizational discipline. In some places, even honor and truthfulness are casualties. Perhaps a university is but a reflection of the disharmony and distrust now gripping the wider society. A loyal nostalgia for university values whispers to us that the university should have done better than this.

Sociologists a generation from now will no doubt come up with their panoply of explanations for this phenomenon. But one line of argument will most certainly be an exploration of white-male guilt in the university community. This sense of guilt has turned out to be of larger dimensions and deeper intensity than anyone could have predicted. Psychologists tell us that guilt is an elusive emotion, hard to track down and harder to cure. It seems to have its origin in some faulty perception of where we are in our world and what responsibility we bear for its past and present. Most certainly, guilt can seriously disorient our attempts at sane, intelligent planning for the future.

During the late sixties, it was fashionable for a white faculty member to be seen championing the cause of blacks—not this black or that black, but all blacks regardless of competence. During the early seventies, a similar reflex obeisance was shown toward the Chicano and Puerto Rican, with an equivalent expression of atonement made audible in the institution's corridors and seminar rooms. During the later seventies, it was women's turn to tweak the guilt strings of the ever-present male administrator, appealing to his sense of fairness and in the very appeal implying his need for rehabilitation.[4]

Through it all the white males cowered. They seemed unable to take strong, decisive action in favor of university values and institutional integrity. The fear of lawsuits loomed as a major new element in administrative decisionmaking at the highest levels. Minorities and women—and their lawyers— were all too ready to make an issue of almost anything, because they knew the mood of the university community, the vulturelike appetite of the press, and, indeed, the ambiance of the entire society regarding equity issues were all on their side.

In the face of this changed political climate, white-male university administrators treaded softly. They mollified blacks with contrived black studies programs; they appeased Latinos with specially created jobs in soft-money Spanish-speaking programs; they arranged for secret, unmerited salary increases for the most belligerent women to keep them quiet and out of the courts.

The question one may now ask is this, How much has been given away? Can the university recover from this orgy of appeasement or has the American university surrendered its soul to affirmative action politics?

As the universities of the nation enter the eighties, they are discovering that something has been gained—a more open environment, a new respect for ethnic minorities, a more cosmopolitan hiring ethic. But they are discovering also that something very important has been lost, namely, the integrity of university standards and the sturdiness of academic values. The pandering to militant factions has left a measurable

---

[4]The increased activity of liberationism on our campuses came at a time when the national picture appeared less and less stable. A split developed in the National Organization for Women, with militants and moderates contending for control. The Equal Rights Amendment began running into trouble in the nation's state legislatures, with women themselves leading the opposition. Consciousness-raising, once touted as good for everybody, turned sour and mean.

trace of continuing intimidation. Admission requirements have been irreversibly lowered, the caliber of students accordingly has dropped, course requirements have been weakened, and—sad to say—grading practices are a farce. It is extremely difficult for a professor to fail a student without at the same time developing an exhaustive file of evidence that will hold up in a court of law.

But pendulums do swing. The eighties are destined to exhibit an altered political ambiance. The rumblings of reverse discrimination charges indicate that we are in for another round of lawsuits and court decisions. The outcome of this litigation will tell us much about the future of the higher learning in America. We have heard, confusedly and indecisively, from the Supreme Court on this question; they have given us decisions on Alan Bakke and Brian Weber. But there will be other grievances, other suits, other decisions that hopefully will lead us back to the lost ethic of equal, color-blind treatment and let-the-best-person-win decisionmaking.

Law suits or no, it is possible that white-male guilt will ease as political pressures subside. If the days of shouting and fingerpointing now belong to the past, it is conceivable that the eighties will bring us a steadier, more rational balance of managerial leadership in our colleges and universities. If it does, that will certainly represent the most affirmative of all actions that higher education could take as a response to the unrest and tumult of the seventies.

# SEVEN

# Money: How To Get It, How To Spend It

PROFESSORS have a love-hate relationship with money. On the one hand, as family providers they are as much trapped in the consumership idiocy of modern society as their fellow citizens. They watch TV, read shiny magazines, take in the billboards glaring down on the expressway, and salivate with the best over sleek automobiles, eight-track stereos, and what *Playboy* magazine calls "the pleasure machines." Professors are hooked, like everybody else.

But their craft, they believe, partakes of a loftier motivation, reaching to a higher, nobler place, the world of the mind. Every professor is in one sense a child of Plato, skeptical of the senses, wary of the animal appetites, and oriented like a compass needle to a realm beyond, where only ideas dwell. If, as Emerson noticed a century ago, "Things are in the saddle and ride mankind," imagine what mot of stupefaction might come from his lips were he alive today. The professor knows that the academic life, whatever else it may be, is a ticket out of the conspicuous-consumpton rat race.

In the academy itself, the ambivalence shows a similar face. Except for his or her own salary, the professor imagines that the university runs pretty much on air. Lawns are mowed, buildings are heated and cooled, and the ever-present typewriters clack away day after day in what the professor imagines to be a dollarless apparatus. The professor's world is talking and writing, two quintessentially coin-free media. Precisely because they are cheap in a mercantile sense, they are exquisitely dear in the intellective commerce of academic life.

The administrator, of course, recognizes this fantasyland conjured by the academic mentality. It is familiar and understandable partly because the dean lived there too. But the passage from faculty life to administrative responsibility thrusts a sudden change of perspective: everything a university does now takes on a dollars-and-cents configuration. Talk and thought may be cheap, but the human beings behind them are very, very expensive.

Which is to say that, at the dean level, the primary cost is people. Upward of four-fifths of the cost of running an academic establishment consists of wages and salaries of employees—from file clerks to research professors. The dean's primary task, therefore, is to purchase and deploy what budgetmakers call "personal services" and the time, energy, and special skills they represent. As experienced academic administrators know, this is a more fragile and risky operation than it may appear to the outsider. A bungled appointment of an incompetent assistant professor can tie up thousands of dollars for several years. Worse, a miscalculation in promoting to tenure rank a young scholar who turns out to have already uttered his last original idea can effectively cripple a department's budget for two to three decades!

Money therefore drives the university just as it drives other organizations. But because so high a proportion of the money goes into people, a commodity not susceptible to tight quality control and because the academy is locked into long-term job protection, a tiny misallocation of funds can have enduring, sometimes damaging, effects many years later.

Money also serves, as it does in most other organizations in America, as the primary counter in the reward system. University professors used to eschew the dollar syndrome, insisting that good students, small classes, and time off for research and writing were the chief motivators to top effectiveness. An ambiance of genteel poverty was accepted as the price one paid for the satisfactions of an academic career. But during the fifties and sixties, this pristine posture began to wobble and fold, and the severe inflation of the seventies and eighties finally did it in. Nowadays, most professors still ask for the same nondollar items, but what they really want is more money. During the years from 1972 to 1980, college and university professors in the United States suffered a loss of 13 percent in real income, and the gap between the professor's salary and the Consumer Price Index continues to widen. Moreover, academics are losing ground to individuals in comparable occupations. They "could do very much better financially electing some other profession, such as law, accounting, finance, or business administration." [1]

It is clear, therefore, that the professoriate is hurting. Even when given time off for research, professors see no inconsistency in taking extra jobs outside their university duties to augment their incomes. Moonlighting has, in fact, become a standard feature of the academic economy. Four out of five faculty members have outside income-producing pursuits. During the eighties this supplement is expected to average almost a quarter of a professor's regular institutional salary. [2]

One of the special fiscal problems of university middle management during the eighties will be the increasing tendency of professors to prolong their careers well beyond the conventional retirement age of sixty-five. With national legislation now prohibiting forced retirement at this or an even later age, senior faculty members who are still vigorous in their late sixties—and some who are not—will opt to keep going, to forestall as long as possible the dreaded cutback in

[1] Peggy Heim, "The Economic Decline of the Professoriate in the 1970's," *Current Issues in Higher Education, 1980,* (Washington, D.C.: American Association for Higher Education, 1980), no. 3, p. 17.
[2] *Chronicle of Higher Education* 13, November 17, 1980.

lifestyle imposed by inadequate pensions and social security benefits.

This reluctance to quit, coupled with the traditional tenure system, means that the most highly salaried academic employees can effectively block the institution from replenishing its supply of brains and teaching manpower with younger people, and continue to do so for as many years as it takes the senior faculty to decide to get out. Because of the differential in salary between retirables and new PhDs, each senior professor will now have squatter's rights on the budget equivalent of two to three junior positions, fresh blood that most universities desperately need even in ordinary times.

The university response to this phenomenon could be enhanced inducements to retire, chief of which would be increased pension allotments. But since pension plans are built on actuarial projections, such schemes would take many years to introduce. A possible compromise would be fractional retirement in which a senior professor would cut back to 75 percent or 50 percent of salary for the final five years, with a corresponding lessening of duties. This would have the effect of releasing at least some funds for the employment of new PhDs emerging from the graduate schools.[3]

\* \* \*

Of the three basic services of a university—teaching, research, and service—teaching always emerges as the primary factor in money allocations. Which is to say that meeting classes and instructing students is expected to be the central task of the faculty, and, indeed, the reason for hiring a faculty in the first place. The fact that teaching is hard to evaluate or that promotion policy should place greater emphasis on teaching skill is of no overriding concern to the budget-maker. What is needed is a person in a classroom engaged in

[3]Delayed retirement is examined in *The Report of the Consortium on Financing Higher Education Study on Faculty Retirement: An Overview,* available from the Consortium, 238 Main St., Cambridge, Mass. 02142.

teaching as many students as possible. The greater the number—sometimes up to five hundred in a lecture hall—the lower the unit cost of producing semester- or quarter-hour credits, which represent the basic commodity the university is selling.

Coordinately, the base income of a university comes from student tuition fees, which are proportionate to the number of credits purchased. Of course, the student, through fees, pays only a fraction of the cost of his education, ranging from 30 percent in large public or well-heeled private institutions up to 80 or 100 percent in small-endowment, private entrepreneurial institutions. But whatever the percentage, the revenue from the customers is always considered the starting point for budget design. In the seventies and eighties, this pecuniary focus on students, or more precisely on semester- or quarter-hour credits generated by students, has led to the general concept of *enrollment-driven budgets*. This phrase implies not only that credit-based tuition revenue shall be considered first but also, more comprehensively, that the cost of educating a student for one credit, whatever it may be, shall serve as the basic counter in deciding who gets what throughout the campus. To standardize this measure for all campus units, most institutions have established what is known as the FTE or *full-time equivalent student*. The standard full load of a student, let us say, is 16 semester hours or 15 quarter hours per term. The registrar's office adds up all the credits for which students in a given college have registered, then divides this sum by 16 or 15, and arrives at a figure representing the number of full-time equivalent students being taught by that college. This, then is the basis upon which budget allotments are made to that college for the succeeding year.

The FTE concept has, of course, also been applied to the supply side of university bookkeeping, namely, the faculty manpower available for teaching. If a full teaching load is, say, 12 semester hours, the business office totes up all the credits for which students have registered, divides by 12, and arrives at a figure representing the number of full-time faculty required to cover those classes. The size of a faculty, therefore, is customarily expressed in terms of FTE faculty units, even though the actual headcount of faculty may be much larger, with some engaged in nonteaching activities.

The student FTE provides a working description of the size of the institution in enrollment terms, a figure that conveys a gross measure of the magnitude of the budgeting environment. During the seventies, total college and university enrollment reached a peak of about 12 million or about six percent of the total population. With about $4,000 a year being spent on each student, higher education thereby became for the first time a $50-billion industry before the eighties began. As projections had predicted, toward the end of the seventies enrollments began to level off and in some places decline, ushering in a retrenchment period in some institutions that may last well into the eighties. In a kind of persistent, pernicious exhibit of Parkinson's Law, it was discovered that as enrollments started downward in the late seventies, the total spending continued upward.[4] Part of this was certainly due to inflation, but it is likely that another part was attributable to the increasing bureaucratization of the higher education industry itself.

The FTE unit, when coupled with the general concept of the enrollment-driven budget, provides academic budget planners with a quantitative tool with which to rationalize a university's operations. Indeed, so central is the FTE arithmetic that the other two main outputs of a university—research and service—are customarily expressed in FTE terms. For example, in order to engender research activities on a campus, the dean may arrange for a faculty member's release from a portion of the FTE faculty load formula. Thus, instead of funding research by calculating its yield or assessing its value—neither of which can be expressed in quantitative terms—the academic middle manager relieves the faculty member of a third or a half of his or her teaching

<hr/>

[4] A study from the National Center for Education Statistics, as reported in the *Chronicle of Higher Education*, August 25, 1980, p. 11.

load, assigning this person instead to research and scholarly endeavors and to the writing of books and articles. The classes of students left uncovered are assigned to other members of the faculty not engaged in research or to ad hoc academic employees hired just for this purpose. These temporary, one-shot teachers are typically drawn from the cadre of teaching assistants, lecturers, and instructors lingering in the shadows of the university, and can be hired for rates far lower than the unit costs of the research-bound professor. Thus, if the professor's research project salary stipend is to be underwritten by an outside agency, the dean can "save" some dollars in the exchange and deploy these funds elsewhere in the organization. Such budget flexibility is obviously of great value to the middle manager, and it is therefore not untypical for university deans to make considerable but judicious use of this special form of academic captive labor.

Being released from teaching duties for research and writing is generally regarded as a reward. But it is always offered with some *quid pro quo* expectation that some research products will flow from it. Sometimes this gift of time yields nothing, in which case the dean would be well advised to decline any future request from that individual for load relief. At other times, the faculty member makes good use of these extra hours in the work year and may, under productive circumstances, become a research entrepreneur in gaining still additional funding or widening the scope of his or her research endeavor. For the truly dedicated research scholar, at least in the early stages of a career, it is probably true that released time has no measurable effect one way or the other on research productivity. The genuinely curious, inquisitive mind will pursue these interests even with a full teaching load. The dean should cultivate this motivation and reward this extra effort with future released time and other budgetary lagniappe available for dispensation—travel money, computer time, a full-time secretary.

In sum, salary items in a budget can be, for managerial

purposes, converted into FTE faculty load units, and these in turn can be manipulated, rearranged, and orchestrated to further the work of the entire organization. What has just been said of released time for research activities holds true also of the service area, although the equivalence of effort is somewhat harder to quantify. A professor engaged in community activities, let us say, is heavily involved in assisting a nonuniversity agency in developing a program for the neighborhood, or a professor in the technological sciences has been asked to donate his expertise to a municipal agency to solve a special problem. If the hours to be devoted to this extramural enterprise can be calculated and if the activity will bring sufficient credit to the university, the dean may see fit to release this professor from a certain percentage of his or her teaching load. In this case, however, the service "product" is elusive and virtually undefinable. Does the neighborhood get its program or the agency get its solution? If so, how much of this achievement can be traced to the participation of the professor? In a crass but perhaps more honest formulation, how much public relations mileage can the college and the university get from donating this professor's time? If the institution can gain politically, the dean can afford to make the donation.

During the late sixties and seventies, universities particularly in the big cities came under enormous pressure to provide an "outreach" to citizens living in the surrounding areas. As noted in chapter 5, no one was quite sure how to go about doing this, especially in hostile, emotionally charged situations. The ostensible demand was for programs for minorities, but in too many cases this customarily translated into jobs for the poor. This in turn led to an agonizing concern: what jobs are there in a university that can be handled by poor, usually undereducated, individuals? As it turned out, there weren't very many, so jobs had to be created—counselors, tutors, advisors, small-group instructors. To fill these jobs, persons were to be recruited from the minority group itself and given charge of students only of that group. To fund these artificially created positions, budget pressure built up to divert funds from the conventional, education-related activities of the university.

Most universities soon learned, however, that there is a limit to this reallocation strategy, so they turned to external sources for the funding of these special programs. As a consequence, there developed during this period what might be called the *politics of funding*, in which the social interests and ideological guilt of government agencies and philanthropic foundations became new targets for revenue. At first the universities took the initiative in this enterprise, putting their neophyte grantsmen to work studying the brochures and portfolios of prospective funding outlets. If the rhetoric in these promotional documents voiced a concern for the plight of blacks, Hispanics, or native Americans and signaled a general desire to help, then university officers formed committees to draft proposals to fit these funding aspirations. Proposals eventually in hand, the grantsmen would begin making their rounds to deliver their pitch to the agencies and foundations.

It soon became evident, however, that all of this background preparation was not really necessary. The agencies and foundations themselves had independently developed an agenda of funding in which minority programs customarily received high priority. During the late seventies, therefore, the agencies and foundations became entrepreneurs of funding on their own, seeking out universities that were in a position to spend their money for them. These external organizations came to appreciate the fact that funneling funds through a university on behalf of minority groups would look good in an annual report. Out of this was born a kind of fail-safe form of philanthropy. If things went well in the hostile ghettos and barrios, the foundation or government bureau could take the credit, winning both friends and votes. If things went badly, the agency could blame it on bumbling academics "who don't know anything about the real world."

With the arrival of the eighties, soft-money budgeting has

become a side industry of its own. Grantsmanship is established as a high-visibility skill in the university, and in some institutions it is overtly recognized as a fourth credential (along with teaching, research, and service) in promotion and tenure considerations. If grantsmanship has been institutionalized in the university, it has also been institutionalized at the other end of the money pipeline, namely, the federal agencies, state offices, and to a lesser extent the foundations. Federal agencies in particular have discovered that the nation's universities represent an extended arm for their own work. This is especially true of research-oriented units such as the National Science Foundation, the National Institutes of Mental Health, and the National Institute of Education. These and other Washington-based bureaus develop their own research programs and then publish and disseminate what are known as RFPs (requests for proposals). Such documents announce what kinds of research studies are wanted and eligible for funding, and they spell out the detailed specifications that must be met in order to obtain favorable consideration.

Studying the RFP and deciphering its contents, the university grantsman begins the arduous but heady task of proposal writing, developing a research investigation idea and explaining in detail how he or she intends to gather the wanted information. The primary object, of course, is to catch the attention of the funding body and particularly its stable of proposal readers who will make the basic recommendations. But a strong secondary motivation is to design a research project that will lead to journal articles, perhaps even books, which in turn can be cashed in later at promotion time.

Ordinarily the granting agency does not specify a dollar figure that the proposal writer is to aim at; instead, the proposer, with the assistance of other university officers, is expected to submit a project budget, explaining what the research effort is going to cost in terms of professor time, travel, secretarial services, computer time, and graduate assistants. This budget then becomes one of the variables considered by the agency's review committee in judging the overall caliber of the entry. As in other contract-letting situations, the lowest bid, other things being more or less equal, has the advantage.

In the real world of grantsmanship, however, things are rarely equal. Sometimes the granting agency knows in advance which university should get the grant. Perhaps the institution in question has done a good job on a similar project earlier or is especially equipped with faculty expertise to conduct the investigation. Or, sad to say, a university may be singled out in advance as a prospective grant winner for political reasons—a high-ranking congressman or senator has been leaning on the agency to do something for his or her district. To maintain the appearance of fairness, the agency must disseminate the RFP to the higher education community and to private enterprise research institutes and think tanks. But when the ultimate winner in the competition is known in advance, the dean and the proposal writers refer to the RFP as "wired." The question now is whether to put a lot of energy into the proposal-writing effort. Suspicions may, of course, prove false, in which case the institution would suffer if it did not submit an entry. But if the grant turns out to have been wired, a large block of faculty time and energy would have been for naught, a budget waste no institution can ever fully recoup. After making discreet, unofficial phone calls and decoding the gossip of colleagues and acquaintances around the country, the dean makes the critical decision whether or not to commit faculty manpower to the proposal-writing effort.

In the university of the eighties, the RFP thus becomes a tantalizing letter from Santa Claus, an invitation to enter a kind of lottery with significantly high stakes. In most grant budgets a major item of surpassing interest to the dean is the category of overhead, variously figured (depending on the agency and the nature of the grant) at from 8 percent to 70 percent of the salaries and wages portion of the negotiated final contract. This money is intended to cover administrative costs, office space, heat, light, use of facilities, and other support factors that are difficult to cost out precisely and, therefore, are lumped together for convenience. The dean of course works for the highest percentage possible, since this money is not earmarked and can be deployed in areas even outside that of the grant activity itself. Sometimes the vice-president's office takes a slice off the top for general university use, but the bulk of this money usually lands in the dean's office and is used to provide extra stenographic services or travel allotments to other professors. From a budgetary standpoint, the overhead stipend provides the academic middle manager with one of the few possibilities for discretionary decisionmaking in the college's fiscal affairs.

It is obvious that the prospect of outside money sets up enormous temptations for university administrators. As noted earlier, funds from a large grant can ease the pain of budget squeeze. Moreover, with this money the university's research sector, traditionally starved out by enrollment-driven-budget thinking, can develop and flourish. But university officers are coming to realize that they may be getting too much of a good thing. Constantly fondling RFPs out of Washington becomes a kind of disease. It puts the university in the position of always bending its own programmatic priorities to fit the needs of other people. The university discovers that it must sell at least a part of its soul to keep solvent.

But worse than this, federal grants increasingly come with strings attached. The long arm of the national government begins to meddle in the affairs of the academy. Federal agencies such as the Occupational Safety and Health Administration or the Equal Employment Opportunity Commission can threaten to cut off funds if their regulations and guidelines are not satisfied. And the unfunny joke is that these very regulations are themselves often in conflict.

For this reason some institutions are edging away from the grantsmanship strategy of fiscal survival. Hope College in

Michigan refuses all federal assistance. If Basic Opportunity Grants (BOG) to students are ruled by the courts as assistance to the institution, then Hope officers have decided to surrender these also, even though the loss of this tuition assistance will mean a threatened loss of students. In similar fashion, but with higher stakes, the University of Georgia and the University of California at Berkeley in the early 1980s became entangled with affirmative action agencies seeking to enforce compliance through the cancellation of federal contracts.

In spite of these warnings, the grantsmanship industry is now operating at full throttle in American higher education. Whatever one might think about federal spending levels and the persistence of deficit budgets at the national level, there is indeed a federal trough (sometimes referred to as "the public tit") to which the universities and their middle managers are inclining. Some do it for survival in an epoch of retrenchment, some to enhance what they already have. But for all, the competition is stiff, and the most powerful universities with their sophisticated faculties are clearly working from a position of strength in the funding scramble.

\* \* \*

The heart of the money game eventually comes down to budgetmaking, an activity that can be considered both a science and an art. To the layman it is difficult to understand how it could be such an arcane subject; all you do is list the things you need, the people you want to employ, the travel you want to reimburse, add it up and that's the budget. In the history of budget theory, this comes close to the conventional wisdom and is generally referred to as the *incremental strategy*. This procedure assumes that what the organization has been doing in the past is worth doing and should continue. The budgetmaker simply designates those items in the budget which should be expanded and offers reasons for doing so. If the reasons are accepted, the increments are provided and the budget is set.

Another strategy, similar in approach but more judgmental, is called the *priority strategy*. The budgetmaker is asked to place a value on the various items in the budget and to defend how each activity contributes to the goals and objectives of the organization. The result of this valuational analysis is a rank ordering of activities from most important to least important. Understandably, when addressing subordinates—e.g., department heads and project directors—the dean is inclined to focus on the least important items in the college's departmental subbudgets. The question is natural: can any of these items be discontinued or phased out in favor of more pressing needs elsewhere? But for the same reasons, when addressing superiors, the dean seeks to divert attention from the least important items in the collegewide budget and encourages the impression that everything is important. Sometimes it works, and sometimes it doesn't.

During the early seventies, in the euphoria of expanding budgets and a dizzying encouragement to try new and costly academic adventures, the dean's job was largely to keep the dollars flowing; in these circumstances, the above two strategies served very well in rationalizing the budget process. But by the late seventies, this cornucopian condition was abruptly reversed, and most institutions found themselves short both on revenue-producing students and on income-producing legislative appropriations. There was also a temporary lull in the soft-money market, foundations grew more wary of waste watchdogs, and government agencies felt the cold winds of Proposition-13 thinking. In a period of stabilization or threatened retrenchment, more stunning, attention-getting strategies were clearly needed.

One of these has come to be called *zero-based budgeting*, an idea that is disarmingly simple. To each dean goes a message from the academic vice-president: "Suppose your allotment for the next fiscal year were zero. What are the absolutely minimum funds you will need to continue with your present program? Are there any programs or people you can do without? Talk it over with your executive committee and report back to me in thirty days." The trauma this kind of communication sets in motion in an academic community is understandably substantial. In one sense this strategy is a variation on the priority procedure, but it goes further: it opens up for the first time the idea that budget cuts are really possible, and, more important, that the dean must assume the burden of proof to prevent them.[5]

A more manageable variation on the zero-based concept is what might be called the *five-and-five method*. Instead of raising a kind of metaphysical question of a zero base, the academic vice-president approaches the problem in a more practical, real-life way and writes to the dean as follows: "Your budget allocation for the current fiscal year is $x$. Suppose your allocation for next year is $x - 5\%$. Please spell out in detail where the 5 percent cut would be made in your current operation and report back to me in thirty days. While you are at it, imagine the impossible, namely, that your allocation for next year is $x + 5\%$; where would you allocate the money? Review all of this with your executive committee and let me have your 95 percent and 105 percent budgets in thirty days."

It is understood, of course, that neither budget figure is to

[5] In recent years a more unorthodox and far-reaching budget theory has been advanced: PPBS or Planning-Programing-Budgeting Systems. The traditional budget (incremental, priority, or zero-based) describes only what things are purchased—the number of professors, administrators, secretaries; the number of typewriters and copying machines; the allotment for audio-visual equipment, paper, pencils, and erasers. It does not say anything about the need for these things or, more important, about how they contribute to the purposes of the institution. Instead, so argue the PPBSers, let the budgetmaker start with the purposes of the institution: instruction of students, production of research results, service to the community. Then cost out each of these items in dollar terms. For example, how many dollars are required to instruct 1,000 freshmen in English composition up to an acceptable level of writing ability? How many dollars will yield 100 pages of scholarly articles in refereed journals? If the purposes of the organization can be specified, if the units of work needed to realize those purposes can be detailed, and if the units, in turn, can be given a price tag, then a completely rational budget can be produced. It can be reported that so far PPBS budgeting has not reached very far into the academy, an institution notorious for its resistance to quantification. For a clear-headed analysis of PPBS in educational situations, see Dale Mann, *Policy Decisionmaking in Education* (New York: Teachers College Press, Columbia University, 1976).

be taken as an institutional forecast for next year. Instead, the academic vice-president is, in effect, psyching out the dean to see where his or her priorities actually lie. In both the five percent cuts and the five percent add-ons the inner working of a dean's mind can be plumbed for telltale signs on budget soft spots and solid priorities. With this knowledge, the central administration can go to work on the serious business of rearranging funds for the whole institution. The five-and-five device offers the dean some flexibility in evaluating the college under his or her direction; but, more important, it offers the vice-president a concrete, line-item map complete with red arrows pointing to the spots where the knife should be placed for the first slice. Instead of having to reach down into a college budget on his own, the vice-president can say to the dean: "Here, let's get rid of this; you suggested it yourself!"

There is no question that budget cutting is the most disagreeable part of an administrator's life. It is especially painful if it requires the severance of capable individuals or the cutting off of promising young careers. A dean, like other administrators, will customarily squeeze out every other non-personnel item in the budget before beginning the agonizing task of trimming dollars from the personal-services category. Even incompetents are reluctantly let go, because their departure may also mean the departure of a position, a line-item in the budget, something very difficult to recapture once it is gone. An empty line is prima facie evidence to a vice-president that a college is overstaffed.

If the dean can turn the trick of removing the person without simultaneously endangering the line itself, budget cutting can become a kind of mathematical art form. Sometimes the dean can obtain a voluntary resignation by judicious leaning on the individual in question, i.e., issuing disagreeable teaching assignments, withholding favors, or delivering the unequivocal message of a zero salary increase.

If these measures fail, the modern dean may repair to

116

the institutional promotion and tenure apparatus. As the eighties begin, institutions of higher education are continuing their efforts to recover from the excesses of leniency allowed to occur during the seventies. Hiring and promotion standards are on their way back up to where they used to be. Tenure is reclaiming its lost position as a mark of academic excellence. In an epoch of tenure glut—the piling up of unmovable, superannuated professors—the dean and college's promotion and tenure committee can afford to be rigorously tough in applying the traditional criteria for academic performance.

In a Machiavellian setting it is even possible for a dean to wipe out whole departments, if their dissolution is necessary for the survival of the remainder of the college. It is not unheard of for a dean to share this feeling of fiscal unease with the senior professors on the faculty, suggesting that they "look very carefully at individuals in Department X." Can the college afford to carry them through this period of budget shortfalls? If the dean can exert political influence on promotion and tenure professors, explaining that their own welfare may be affected by the continuation of Department X, it is possible that they will get the message and turn the screw with somewhat greater force.

When heads roll, the presumption is that they are incompetent heads and that they should roll. But when whole departments are cashiered, there is every likelihood that some competent people may get caught in the machinery of evaluation. It is these individuals for whom the dean's greatest managerial ingenuity must be saved. Are they capable of assuming other assignments in the college once their department has been wiped out? Can their special expertise be adapted to another program elsewhere in the university? Are they capable of being recycled into new fields or new careers by taking a sabbatical year off for retraining? Faculty renewal and development is certain to be a major concern of deaning in the eighties. Accordingly, the American Association for Higher Education has turned its attention, through many publications, to this question.[6] The salvaging of highly educated, intellectual human resources is not only a humanitarian thing to do; it is also a practical necessity for institutions continually in search of competent manpower in an age of budget squeeze.

[6]See, for example, monograph 2, "Faculty Career Development," and monograph 7, "PhDs in Nonacademic Careers: Are there good jobs?", in *Current Issues in Higher Education, 1979* (1979).

# EIGHT

# Governance: Running the Store

A DEAN has two constituencies: the faculty below and the academic vice-president[1] above. From a purely political standpoint, the art of deaning is measured by how well these two constituencies are stroked, cajoled, cultivated, and kept in line. Although this balancing act is not unique in organizational life, there are features in the middleness of the academic middle manager that are typically not found elsewhere.

College professors are fiercely, idiosyncratically independent in their daily behavior. The nature of their work engenders a special pride in *not* being responsive to institutional discipline. Thus, they represent a constituency that is almost purely political in character; that is to say, it cannot be commanded or led. Rather, it is merely organized and made to feel as if it were being led, but by the initiatives and cohesion of its own membership, not by a dean. The faculty's motivations must be harnessed in somewhat the same way as a

[1] In some universities, this individual is called *dean of faculties*, *provost*, or in smaller institutions *academic dean*. In any case, this person is typically the number two executive on the campus, with specific responsibility for academic affairs. See figure on page 9.

politician coaxes and mobilizes public opinion in a voting district.

The academic vice-president may not fully appreciate this if he or she has reached the vice-presidential echelon without having previously served as a dean. Deaning bestows a special, indefinable loss of innocence that no other academic experience can quite make up for; it leads to an awakening that comes only with on-the-job apprenticeship. Accordingly, one should be wary of superiors who have not themselves experienced the pressure cooker of a deanship or its equivalent. Without it their administrative education is incomplete.

The academic vice-president, whether so educated or not, represents the dean's other constituency and embodies a more familiar hierarchical prototype. He or she speaks for the president and board of trustees, issues instructions, and gives orders. In these activities, the vice-president exercises functions that are directly related to organizational command and are, therefore, quite unlike those of a dean.

Because of the nature of their work, university professors are not expected to be familiar with this side of university administration. Indeed, it is this chain-of-command mentality that is the primary object of their scorn. Since it does not relate directly to teaching and research, the hierarchy seems somehow outside the zones of professoring. As professors go about their daily routines, they sense that a higher boss commands somewhere above, but they imagine the dean to be as free as they are in dealing with this next level of authority.

Thus, a discontinuity of expectation exists between the faculty, who live in a kind of do-your-own-thing world, and the academic vice-president, who lives in a superior-to-subordinate accountability world. The dean, with one foot in each, is a bridge that is expected to join these two worlds.

To change the image, the dean is a Janus, facing two directions simultaneously. In homelier terms, the dean is in the sometimes awkward but potentially creative position of serving two masters, each of whom works from a different premise of organizational response. In large part the middle-management job consists in explaining these two spheres to each other and providing the corporate interlock between them.

Some years ago an individual held a joint appointment between two colleges on an Eastern campus. He was officially on the payroll of the Graduate School of Education, but his professional assignment—his "detached duty," so to speak— was coordinator of teacher education in a semiautonomous undergraduate college in the same university. When asked how it felt to work for two deans, his response revealed an intriguing organizational imagination: "I tell each of them that I belong to the other one. It seems to work."

Such a stratagem is theoretically possible in the Janus circumstance of a dean, except in this case the two constituencies are more organically connected. When the situation tightens and options narrow, the academic vice-president expects a dean to deliver a faculty to his side of an issue. Likewise, faculty members expect a dean to fight for their rights and prevail on their behalf with the vice-president. The dean belongs to both camps but in a functional, chain-link way. He or she must act in such a way as to keep the two constituencies moving more or less in the same direction.

Because of this vital symbiosis between the two poles of a dean's life, his stature with one is a necessary function of his stature with the other. A vice-president's confidence in a dean's judgment depends largely on how well the dean can mobilize a faculty in support of the vice-president's goals or how energetically the dean pursues collegiate development along lines demanded by the central administration. Likewise, the faculty's confidence in a dean is influenced by the vice-president's rapport with the dean. If that rapport appears strong and supportive, the faculty's confidence is fortified. But if that rapport is shaky and if the vice-president overrules the dean frequently or permits faculty end-runs around the dean to higher officers, the dean's position with his own colleagues is made increasingly untenable.

All these built-in difficulties of middle management are commonplace in all organizations. Yet in university life they are magnified by the special peculiarities of academic loyalties. A professor's career is conducted largely before a national audience. He uses his institution as a platform from which his findings or ideas can be displayed to those who really count, namely, external critics. Accordingly, a professor has only the most casual commitment to his home base. His wallet is sustained here, but his heart lies elsewhere.

Quite to the contrary, a vice-president has customarily forsaken professorial work permanently and has opted for an administrative career. The welfare of the institution as such is therefore this person's first consideration. His life, his ego, his sense of worth are all tied up with his university. As a member of an administrative team, his first loyalty is not only expected by but is also willingly given to the institution he not unsentimentally considers his.

The dean is the vital linkage between these disparate modes of loyalty. He or she must respect a faculty member's orientation to an external audience and must, in fact, encourage and fortify it. Indeed, the reputation of an entire college over which a dean presides is ultimately measured by those outside the campus walls. But, while urging this outward look, the dean must, on the faculty's behalf, turn inward to his superiors and share in looking after the institution's total welfare. As a member of the administration, the dean is a critical cog in the campus hierarchy and perforce a "company man."

What ultimately separates a dean from his faculty is, therefore, the trappings of this institutional role—not the company-man syndrome as such but what that term implies, namely, *responsibility for the institution.* The term *line officer* signifies this special role. In traditional management theory, the word *line* understandably carries a heavy freight of meanings. But in an organization such as a university, where corporate discipline counts for so little, a line role becomes much more important and at the same time more tenuous and brittle.

A dean may continue to see himself as just another member of the faculty, a first-among-equals sort of person. But in the act of deaning, the dean must enter a separate life, the world of accountability. Faculty members are singularly free of this pressurized condition and are, therefore, unacquainted with its emotional significance. They can say what they please any time, letting the consequences of their words or conduct roll on to whatever good or damage may result.

Line responsibility engenders line authority, namely, an arena of decisionmaking singled out and designated as belonging to the position of dean. Within this zone, the dean's judgments are unquestioned and final, protected from incursions from below and above. A dean can usually handle challenges from faculty members. It is the incursion from above that creates the most mischief.

In universities, and perhaps through all organization life, this is one of the hardest lessons to learn. There is the constant temptation for the vice-president to reach down in the chain of command and exert his or her own will by steering a subordinate—in this case, the dean—toward one particular option. But whenever this is done, even with the best of motives, it sets in motion several crippling tendencies. First it undercuts the dean's effectiveness in managing the total number of variables under his or her jurisdiction. From a purely practical standpoint it weakens the dean's ability to arrive at future decisions and make them stick. Finally, since it contradicts the very rationale on which the chain-of-command model is constructed, such second-guessing of a dean eventually weakens the vice-president's ability to govern. By such behavior he or she sends out the signal to all other deans that their judgments, even in those areas specifically assigned to them, are only tentative and subject to reversal. Under these conditions it is obvious that middle management at the dean level becomes merely a game of passing messages between the faculty and the vice-president, a clerical function more appropriately handled by less expensive personnel.

The wise vice-president does not get drawn into this debilitating game. He sets the dean free with his or her own portfolio, to do with as that person deems best. Although this zone of judgment is not extensive at the middle-management level, it represents that area of administrative functioning which provides the greatest satisfactions. It is in this zone that the special insights, the particular priorities, and eventually the unique power of the dean can be laid upon the entire organization. The dean exploits this confined but precious area to work his or her will on the college-shaping materials at hand. The dean approves certain appointments to the faculty and disapproves others, urges promotions of some individuals but counsels termination for others, pushes some programs and allows others to languish and die, and approves budget allotments to one research project but denies them to another. Finally, with the most decisive weapon, the dean allots large salary increases to the excellent and serves up zero for the unproductive and uncooperative. The cumulative effect of these decisions over the years is to create a college that is an extension of the dean's professional self. A personal stamp, as they say, has been put upon it.

\* \* \*

In analyzing the authority-responsibility nexus, it is important to acknowledge a special complication indigenous to the academic establishment, namely, the presence of a second, more or less parallel, and sometimes competing chain of command, namely, the faculty committee structure. The conventional chain consists of the customary set of officers alluded to above: president, academic vice-president, dean, department head. Along this line, upward and downward, flow the decisions that govern the ordinary operations of the institution. In a university setting, however, special powers have historically been granted to the faculty, specifically those covering the establishment of academic policy. As everyone knows, this term can be expanded to include virtually everything a university does, and for this reason, an aggressive faculty, if well organized, can arrogate to itself a very large sphere of control over a university's managerial apparatus.

As noted, the key to power is organization. This may begin in small ways. A faculty committee is elected by the faculty, let us say, to oversee curriculum development. In the course of its work, it announces a determination to exercise final control of formal course outlines, with the explicit caveat that no administrative officer shall have veto power over its decisions. Or, an elected faculty committee may decide to speak for the faculty in setting admission requirements for students, again with the implied assumption that no administrator shall be permitted to overrule any requirement ratified by the full faculty. The next step may consist of a faculty executive committee's assuming full responsibility for decisions regarding the appointment, promotion, and tenure of faculty members or, in the ultimate quest for power, announcing its determination to control the budget.

Most university line officers would be willing to accommodate to a no-veto policy on such matters as course design and program requirements. These are clearly academic matters in the strictest sense of the term. However, on such questions as admissions requirements, faculty personnel, and budget, it is obvious that wide-ranging consequences are set in motion by an institution's decisions. Accordingly, a line officer is unlikely to allow a faculty decision to become "law" without a thorough administrative review and possible veto. In these cases, an aggressive faculty may press this jurisdictional claim by an intimidating maneuver. They may send word that if any faculty recommendation is overruled or ignored, the dean must appear personally before them to defend the action with an exhaustive detailed accounting and to provide explicit reasons for deviating from the recommended action.

A resourceful dean need not be intimidated by such a request. Although such a requirement tends to discourage an administrator's willingness to contradict his colleagues, it also provides a forum for the dean to articulate his or her goals and priorities and to argue for a more generous, institutionwide perspective when the faculty may have been too narrow and parochial. Such a confrontation also helps the dean smoke out the purely personal motivations of professors and the intramural politics that drives professorial thinking. If managerial prudence dictates a different course, the dean must set it.

The alternate, faculty-powered chain of command may grow and distribute itself throughout all departments and colleges. It represents a kind of shadow government, more or less matching the levels of authority intrinsic to the line chain. The faculty committee apparatus customarily culminates in a faculty senate, a body that in some places takes on the attributes of a combination legislature and court in enacting and reviewing institutionwide policy decisions. The strength of the senate apparatus—the ratio of shadow to substance, if you will—is a direct yield of the organizing ability of the faculty in converting itself into a political unit, that is, the degree of discipline the faculty can engender in its own hierarchy of committees and how well this chain of committees moves together in unison in directing the affairs of the institution.

As the above analysis implies, on some campuses the faculty apparatus is wide-ranging and powerful, well organized from the lowliest departmental committee to the senate executive committee, that tight oligarchy which regularly sits with and shadow governs the president. In such institutions, the very power of this alternate chain of command betrays the presence of a weak and impotent line of administration, one whose policies are either ignored and covertly sabotaged by a cadre of dissident faculty or, coordinately, are not promulgated by the administrative staff until they have received the prior imprimatur of the senate hierarchy.

On other campuses, power remains in the line administration. In these circumstances, the politicizing of the faculty may be feeble and diffuse. The administration, including the deans, either prevents it from developing, co-opts its leaders into administrative staff positions, or, more infrequently, manages affairs so well as to obviate the necessity for it. Weak faculty organization is particularly noted on those campuses with dominant boards of trustees, vigorous central officers, and a tradition of strong leadership at the dean level.

Whether the faculty chain of command is strong or weak depends also on the faculty's priorities. For a faculty governance structure to be successful, large numbers of professors must necessarily forgo the pursuit of their scholarship in favor of campus political activity. Every campus harbors a certain number of these individuals, many of whom know subconsciously by mid-career that they will never make it in the external world of research and scholarship; they opt instead for a life of intramural political maneuvering and influence peddling with their campus colleagues. Their energies are diverted from scholarship, even from teaching, and are consumed with the gamesmanship of organizing likeminded individuals throughout the campus to vote the "right" way, even on trivial issues, in the campus senate.

The relationship between the line and faculty chains of command is one of uneasy liaison. The history of higher education virtually requires that they both exist and do business with one another. But it is equally obvious that since they traverse the same ground and govern the same territory, the opportunities for conflict are frequent and numerous.

Just as the dean has two constituencies, analogously it might be said that the line administration in a university has its two constituencies, namely, the faculty on one side and the board of trustees on the other.[2] If the faculty constituency comes to be represented by a strong and aggressive faculty-based political apparatus, the line administration faces

[2]Other constituencies include, of course, the student body, the students' parents, and the alumni. Because of their transiency, students have always found it difficult to organize politically. Even following the late sixties and early seventies when protest was articulate and visible, they were never able to convert their emotional, campus-newspaper solidarity into continuing political organizations capable of exerting significant influence on governance patterns. Parents and alumni, for their part, are very difficult to organize, and they rarely intrude on governance matters.

strong competition in guiding the institution along lines acceptable to the trustees. In this circumstance, a line dean comes to rely more and more heavily on the team of other line administrators in the echelons above. If this group is wobbly and indecisive, a dean can survive only if he or she is willing to accept the policy directions legislated by the faculty apparatus. Sometimes, with especially weak top-level officers and trustees, the faculty "government" can force line officers from office if the faculty does not like their mode of leadership.

If, on the other hand, the line echelons above are firm and sure-footed in their managerial behavior, they are capable of drawing the entire line hierarchy together as an integrated network of officers who are then in a position to assist one another, and, when necessary, support and defend one another when mischief erupts.

To sum up, the dean operates in a circumstance where middleness has a number of dimensions. First there are the disparate pulls of external and internal loyalties, both of which the dean must identify with and harmonize. Then there exists the tension between the faculty, who can afford to be free-wheeling and independent, and a dean's superiors, who are disciplined to the requirements of institutional responsibility. The dean must understand and respond to both. Finally there is the uneasy dialectic between two competing ladders of authority, the regular line, which is de jure and structural, and the faculty apparatus, which is de facto and political.[3] The dean is the connecting link between the two. As we survey this landscape, we see the difficult yet exciting context in which a dean functions. If faint of heart, he or she can simply get mired in the center of this quicksand of polarities. But the vigorous dean will see the job as a hub of possibilities, where deaning becomes a creative center for bringing these disparate, spirited forces together.

\* \* \*

[3] In a few pages, we shall see that still other agencies have infiltrated the decision-making machinery of the modern university, making life even more difficult for the administrator.

When difficulties multiply and problems mount, the dean's primary constituency turns out to be the vice-president. This is where his appointment came from in the first place, even though with faculty approval, and it is from this office that the primordial line authority of a dean originates. If, therefore, a strong line administration is operating in a university and if that administration is providing vigorous, visible support to the dean, middle management can be conducted with some semblance of order and reason.

Perhaps, however, the surest test of a dean comes when a vice-president who is otherwise supportive nevertheless hands down a policy directive with which the faculty is in strong disagreement. The situation may be further exacerbated if this directive has been decided upon with little or no consultation with the dean or the faculty. As noted earlier the vice-president takes the measure of a dean, in part, by how quickly and how effectively he or she can deliver the vote, that is, convert the demurring faculty as a group to the policy position being enunciated and directed by the vice-president. Here we have a paradigm case of a major confrontation not merely between the dean's two constituencies, but more importantly between two worlds of action where the rationale for the final decision is drawn from two different political logics. In this brokerage capacity a dean's administrative skills are finally counted up. A concrete example may help to illustrate this point.

In line with urban-mission urgencies, the dean and a college faculty devote many months planning a special program to train Spanish-speaking students for teaching positions in bilingual schools. Since the program is to be funded by the federal government, the dean and faculty agree that school personnel, parents of Spanish-speaking children, and community lay persons should be invited to participate in the planning process. With all involved, the proposal is put together, forwarded to Washington, and eventually funded; and the money is remitted directly to the university for handling and disbursement as the primary contracting agent.

Upon award of the grant, federal officers from the Health,

Education, and Welfare Department make known to the university that a condition of the grant is the continued involvement of nonuniversity people as advisers and that the project will continue to be watched closely from Washington, D.C., for ongoing evidence of this participation. Hearing of this, the parents and community lay persons arbitrarily and unilaterally convene and organize themselves into an ad hoc steering committee of twenty individuals to administer the project. As a nod to the university, they agree that one of the twenty can be a member of the faculty. Their announced agenda is to assume direct responsibility for recruiting and admitting students to the program, for designing special Spanish-culture courses, and for selecting instructors.

Understandably this development surprises and troubles the faculty, since it is clearly at variance with the spirit of collaborative planning. As faculty members see it, the committee members are not academically qualified to direct a professional program in teacher education. Moreover, by its initial announcements, the committee intends to push beyond an *advisory* role into a self-proclaimed *executive* role. Faculty members argue strenuously that if this committee is recognized, the faculty must assume responsibility for a teacher preparation program, the control of which they have been forced to surrender to a nonacademic, "pick-up" team of laymen outside the university. In a context of friendly good-will and amiable cooperation, such an arrangement might be possible; but, they contend, in a highly charged political atmosphere, one vote out of twenty is not much to work with. The faculty is restless and angry.

On behalf of the faculty, the dean registers these views directly with the vice-president, making the case that the faculty is the body empowered to conduct teacher-training programs. Accordingly, the dean requests of the vice-president that he use his good offices to dissolve the steering committee in favor of a college faculty committee augmented by duly selected community advisors.

The vice-president hesitates. His office has been under severe political pressure in recent weeks from Latino citizens who have staged stormy meetings, sit-ins, and public picketing against the university, demanding control of all Latino-oriented programs. Citing these inflammatory conditions and heeding the proviso of the federal grants officers, he feels the university must adopt a novel, untried, but potentially creative stance in situations of this sort. Specifically, he contends that the university's primary mission is to increase involvement of community groups in the design of its programs. Because of historical conditions, Latino citizens have been frozen out of higher education in the United States. Here, he argues, is a concrete opportunity to reverse that injustice, to reach out to them for their advice and wisdom, in order directly to bring visible relevance to the university's work. The college, he reminds the dean, has no Latino professors. What better way to bring new insights into the college's professional programs than to capitalize on the availability of Latino parents and community leaders and their open willingness to share their ideas. Accordingly, he instructs the dean to work out an arrangement whereby the faculty and the committee can *share* administrative control of the program, with the faculty making sure that university rules, regulations, and standards are adhered to.

The vice-president forthwith appears at a public meeting of the committee, and in the presence of the dean, endorses its legitimacy and its important role in the overall direction of the program.

The middle-management question is thus posed with startling urgency: how is the dean to persuade a hard-working faculty, embedded in their own perceptions and jealous of their prerogatives, to unbend and try a new relationship?

The dean begins by convening the executive committee of the college and initiates the slow, painful educational process. First, it is important for the faculty to realize that it is impossible at this juncture to pull out of the project. Even though the vice-president has taken liberties with the university's traditional protocols of hegemony over its own programs, it would be politically embarrassing for the college and the university to seem to be withdrawing from such a worthy undertaking. The local newspapers would pounce on such a move. One can imagine the headlines: State University Turns Back on Chicanos!

The dean then articulates the vice-president's arguments in favor of accommodation. It is certainly true that the university and college's stated mission is splendidly consistent with a greater flexibility in this area. More important, the college is in essence being asked by the vice-president to deliver on this pledge, to be on the forward edge of institutional change, and to provide a model of academic innovation and initiative. Although the vice-president did not say so, the dean can interpret his orders to mean a confidence in the college faculty in pulling this off, in blazing a new trail in working collaboratively with external groups. Here, after all, is the new frontier in American higher education.

The dean recognizes the risks involved, but urges an exploratory, experimental angle of approach. He argues that even without effective control of the project, the college and university may be able to learn some new things about bilingual education. Going beyond the vice-president's preoccupation with "mission," the dean suggests a still greater ultimate payoff, namely, a heightened phenomenological awakening to the needs of Latino culture by the university's faculty and administration. Urban mission rhetoric should stress a reverse "bounce," a reciprocal remittance of understanding to the university in the process of serving the community. Through such feedback, the academic community might grow in its perceptions of the needs of urban peoples.

To some professors this litany of arguments may mean little. Preoccupied with their own research with or devoting full energies to their teaching and students, they are unwilling to reach out to new challenges. And when not reaching they are willy-nilly forced into new situations, they are wary of new techniques and novel accommodations. A dean cannot be discouraged by these types. He or she must transcend their library-laboratory-classroom orientation and begin the search for younger, fresher, more pliable partners for the new jobs being thrust upon our colleges and universities. A dean is not merely a spokesman for the institutional mission but, more important, for the vehicle through which professors see what needs doing in society and how their own specialty can be brought to bear on it. In the end the task of academic leadership is to release every power and every skill in the faculty and bring it to its full service to the wider community.

* * *

In considering the relationship of the dean to the governance structure, the preceding commentary has necessarily concentrated on the primary machinery of institutional management. It is important, however, to acknowledge the existence of three other, somewhat ad hoc, outposts of authority that are part of the managerial environment with which a dean must sometimes deal, namely, the university's grievance committee, the local equal-employment-opportunity office, and the A.A.U.P.

The grievance agency, either formal or informal, has been established on most campuses as a method by which individual faculty members may register dissatisfaction with their working conditions. Its creation as a separate entity has been thought necessary because professors may be reluctant to register complaints with their administrative superiors out of fear of reprisal. Too, professors may fear ostracism from their colleagues and are reluctant to utilize the formal faculty committee apparatus, even though some of these committees are specifically charged with responsibility for personnel matters. Thus, in such instances of high paranoia, a faculty member has available a panel of outsiders who have little to do with the inner workings of his or her college and can, it is assumed, cast a more objective eye on the festering trouble. A complaint is filed and the ombudsman process begins its heavy work.

Since this grievance avenue represents another alternate to the regular decisionmaking channels, the directives it produces can seriously multiply the administrative burdens of the middle manager. Essentially, the grievance process, by its very existence, serves to convert an individual professor's disgruntlement into a special case, by which we mean a circumstance idiosyncratic to the complainant and therefore incapable of being illuminated by prevailing guidelines or precedents. Also, in most situations, the features of the complaint are supposedly so individualized as to require secret and confidential handling.

The same is generally true of still another grievance channel represented by the affirmative action bureaucracy. On some campuses it is argued that complaints centering on racial or sexual discrimination should be treated separately. Either the grievance agenda is overly full or the character of complaints is presumed to be outside the competence of the established committees. In any event, here is another class of cases which, by the proliferation of institutional decisionmaking, is referred to a jury outside the regularized apparatus of the organization.

Finally, the American Association of University Professors may occasionally be heard from. Although not supported by university funds, as are the other two, the local chapter of the A.A.U.P. represents yet another channel through which dissatisfactions can be voiced and administrative decisions overturned. Over the years the association has concentrated primarily on the major problems of academic freedom, tenure, and dismissals. However, its local officers are frequently called in by complainants to fortify and support lesser charges of injustice—excessive workload, onerous committee assignments, denial of summer employment—that are leveled against deans and higher officers.

Although these alternate judgmental bodies no doubt have a task to perform, they encourage end runs around the system. The secrecy and closed discussion under which they operate inevitably tend to energize the rumor mill and to provide a forum for gossip and hearsay—corrosive pollutants in any communication network. The existence of these multiple agencies represents a special mode of redundancy, revealing a university's lack of confidence in the probity of its regular channels of complaint, namely, the line administration and the faculty committee apparatus. It is a mark of the academic establishment that it overprovides safeguards for the individual, apparently on the assumption that having more avenues of redress than are actually necessary is the best institutional guarantee of its employees' civil rights.

\* \* \*

From a middle-management standpoint, this surfeit of decisionmakers—vice-president, faculty committee, grievance committee, E.E.O. office, A.A.U.P.—comes to represent a countervailing impediment to sound administrative practice. Everyone is looking over the dean's shoulder, inspecting every decision, challenging every judgment, dismantling every option to verify the reasons lying behind every executive act. In today's environment of wholesale skepticism, an educational administrator spends a sizable proportion of time on the job explaining and defending the decisions he or she made the day before. Although this ritual can be salutary in opening up a closed network of communication, its daily practice—like Chinese water torture—eventually weakens executive resolve. It wears away, bit by bit, the stamina necessary to carry the heavy responsibility that line duty implies.

On some campuses the very act of judgment itself is on trial. This means that the task of deaning, the center of which is judgmental in character, is today in an increasingly weakened condition. Withstanding the "heat in the kitchen" is not all that difficult if a dean can make his or her decisions stick. But if everybody else on a campus is also in the business of deciding, then the dean's role is confounded and diminished.

It is for this reason that deaning has become a transient, gypsy occupation. The average tenure of a dean is approximately four years, indicating either the early onset of managerial weariness or the short-term exasperation threshold of faculties trying to get all their wants satisfied.

On some campuses, survival at the dean's job has been worked out over several years through a strategy of managerial withdrawal. This strategy consists in responding to the multiplicity of decisionmakers on campus by retreating from the arena and letting the faculty speak *ex collegio*. In this mode of administrative style, the dean becomes the instrument of the faculty; he or she acts only with the consensus of the faculty, using the faculty as a screen to hide behind. To change the metaphor slightly, the dean in this circumstance becomes a kind of high-salaried clerk, an executive secretary of an association of professors, keeping the files, convening the committee meetings, and assuming the role of senior staff person to the real decisionmakers, the senior professors.

Where this style of administration is predominant, deaning may not be so gypsy. Quite the contrary, a dean who assumes the executive-secretary role can last indefinitely, so long as the full professors don't start fighting among themselves. And if this group itself has a senior person serving as a power-behind-the-throne regent, the dean may remain indefinitely, until the arrival of a dignified, if uncelebrated, retirement. The collection of deans on a campus embracing this administrative ambiance will resemble a petrified forest of middle executives, themselves banding together into a deanly brotherhood. With group strength they can usually make life miserable for the vice-president. In such institutions, it is the vice-presidency that becomes the gypsy occupation.

\* \* \*

Notwithstanding the overabundance of decisionmakers or the survival devices endemic to the job, the dean of the eighties will confront problems of governance that are new to this position. They represent spheres of "running the

136

store" not hitherto encountered in the recent history of American higher education.

Political activity from outside groups, those who made a career of intimidation and mau-mauing, has noticeably subsided on the modern campus. The militancy of faculties remains, but it has now turned inward to their own welfare within the institution. Accordingly, faculty unionism is now either already here or an imminent reality throughout the higher education community. It is understandable that in a period of unchecked inflation, the working person at any level and in any calling will escalate efforts to protect his or her position in the economy. For doctors, lawyers, dentists, architects, indeed, the full gamut of self-employed professionals, the answer clearly lies in charging more for one's services. But because university professors are employees of organizations, trapped by the inherent weakness of the employee status, their response to the economic squeeze cannot be individual action but some form of group bargaining.

It goes without saying that such collective action, because it originated in the blue-collar labor movement, has always been regarded by the intellectual, definitely white-collar professor as undignified and somehow degrading to the professional role. But this haughtiness is rapidly giving way to a pragmatism that most of us can understand. If one is not to be left out in the scramble for dollars, one must join with colleagues, whatever the collar, and press for a fair share of the pie.

Over the last forty years, three organizations—the American Federation of Teachers, the National Education Association, and the American Association of University Professors—have been pretending to the role of organizational voice of the university teacher. The A.F.T. has traditionally been thought too closely tied to the factory laborer to be a suitable representative of the academic class. The N.E.A., on the other hand, built its power through identification with the elementary and secondary schools of the nation and has been unfamiliar with and somewhat indifferent to the special problems and aspirations of the higher education community. Finally, the A.A.U.P. from its inception has concentrated on the relatively narrow, albeit critical, issues of academic freedom and tenure and has been reluctant to enter the rough-and-tumble of labor negotiations and the calling of strikes. So, each organization comes to the higher-education organizing task with somewhat less than impressive credentials.

Nevertheless, unionization through all these groups has gained momentum during the seventies. At the outset of the eighties, each of the three has sharpened its organizational tools and is ready for a full-scale onslaught on what many regard as the last bastion of the "company-town" mentality, the nation's colleges and universities. So far the A.F.T. and the N.E.A. have exhibited the greatest success at the junior-college and community-college level, but they are pressing forward into the four-year schools.

The A.A.U.P. is rapidly losing its milquetoast timidity and has already scored some impressive victories. As the seventies came to a close, the A.A.U.P. chapter at a large midwestern university developed enough muscle to call a faculty strike and effectively shut down the institution for six days. The issues, as one might expect, were the academic equivalent of the familiar bread-and-butter demands of an earlier day. The faculty was asking for a 12½ percent salary increase to be spread over two years. The administration offered 6 percent. During the strike, classes were effectively shut down while the two negotiating teams tried to reach an agreement. Arbitration was tried, but it was unsuccessful.[4] During the lengthy negotiations, the education dean was asked to fill in for a regular member of the management team. At a cocktail party his wife excused his absence by remarking that he was really on the faculty's side but had an obligation, as an administrator, to do his duty for the institution.

This casual aside may sum up, better than any formal

[4] For this account, I am indebted to Professor Kathy Borman of the University of Cincinnati.

138

statement, the peculiar posture a dean is expected to assume when professor unionism arrives on campus. The dean is a member of both camps—a professor in good standing sharing all of the motivations and insecurities of the professorial ranks, but at the same time a member of management and committed to the welfare of the total organization. The middleness of the dean's position as middle manager is perhaps nowhere so starkly portrayed as in union contract negotiations.

Moreover, the end result of contract negotiations, i.e., a contract, may have an ambiguous impact on the dean's job. On the one hand, a faculty's morale should improve whenever there is overt proof that they can assume greater control over their own economic welfare. To have a union to speak for one on salary questions is to remove one more irritant from the conditions of the workplace, and a dean should be able to reap some benefit from this heightened sense of satisfaction. On the other hand, a contract by definition removes critical decisionmaking powers from the dean's hands; he or she is no longer in a position to make judgments as to the work assignments or the salary of members of the faculty. Having lost this last remaining authority means that the dean no longer controls the incentive apparatus of the organization. As one observer put it: "Unionism of professors makes the dean's job a lot easier; he doesn't have to worry about salary hassles any more!"

Labor negotiations are unfamiliar ground for most academics. They lack experience in the rough-and-tumble of bartering and trading. Their cerebral composure is rattled by having to slug it out at the money level with a bureaucratic adversary. Accordingly, many professors, especially those of the A.A.U.P. type, find the whole exercise somehow unsavory and intellectually undignified. One observer, commenting offhandedly about the current situation, suggested that although the A.A.U.P. has grown out of the bowels of academia, those institutions which now have the A.A.U.P. as their bargaining unit experience total chaos at the bargaining table. University administrators who have to face collective bargaining would much prefer to negotiate with the A.F.T., since they can regard it as a straightforward union that at least has the presence of mind not to mix rhetoric, philosophy, canned jargon, and paranoia into one bag without understanding the difference.

But the niceties of discourse and due attention to what is known among negotiating experts as "the philosophy of the table,"[5] have been thrown into a cocked hat by the Supreme Court of the United States. In a landmark decision on Yeshiva University early in the eighties, the Court called into question the very legitimacy of faculty unionism and hence the faculty's right to bargain with their employers. In this decision the Court found that in so-called *mature* universities the faculty are managerial employees, that they are part of the governing apparatus of the institution, and that hence they are not protected in their organizing efforts by the National Labor Relations Act.[6] The Court left in doubt the status of nonmature institutions in which the professors more nearly resemble teachers in a junior college or high school situation and do not participate in the governance role. Also ambiguous is the organizing status of all nontenured professors for whom, it is obvious, there is no governance responsibility. Are these individuals—instructors, assistant professors, teaching assistants, research associates, and lab technicians—prohibited from organizing? It is predicted that a decade of lawsuits will be required to answer these questions.

\* \* \*

A well known Steinberg *New Yorker* cartoon shows an executive addressing a subordinate. The balloon above is sprin-

[5] For this phrase and for special help on this topic, I am indebted to Thomas A. Emmet, assistant to the president of Regis Educational Corporation of Denver, Colorado, and a widely consulted expert on academic unionism.

[6] See Edward J. Burke, "Yeshiva: An End to Faculty Unions?" *Change Magazine* 12 (April 1980): 15–16.

kled with lots of little yeses, showering their benign glow all over the friendly little conference. But all of the yeses have formed themselves into a very large word, *no*. For those who have inhabited the dean's chair, the essence of the dean's task is to say no when necessary in a warm and affirmative way.

A dean, of course, says yes much more often than no. But it happens that, like all of us, university professors remember the nos longer and with more emotional affect than they remember the yeses. Sooner or later, the dean has had to say no at least once to every member of the faculty. With each succeeding no—and they come with increasing frequency and heartbreak in times of retrenchment—the dean's support base gradually diminishes.

Some "park-bench" students of deaning have thought it possible to convert these phenomena into something resembling a law of deanly survival. One such formula, originating with a midwestern dean of education, specifies that the maximum effective life of a university dean is seven years. Every dean comes into office with a pile of chips. As decisions are made day by day and week by week, more and more members of the faculty perceive themselves disadvantaged by the dean's actions. Accordingly, with each decision, the dean must surrender a few chips of good will or executive credibility. The pile gradually gets down, and at the end of the seventh year it is gone. According to this analysis it is theoretically possible for a dean to hang on beyond the seven-year terminus, but his or her decisionmaking effectiveness is so weakened by the erosion of support that leadership is no longer possible.

When, or even before, this point is reached, a dean would do well to begin active consideration of the act of resigning. There is, in the arcane rituals of the higher learning, a certain choreography connected with administrative resignations. It is important, for example, to choose one's own time to resign. More important, it is imperative for the middle manager—or any administrator—to resign for the right reasons, making certain that it can be declared publicly as a vol-

141

untary act. It also helps if a matter of principle is involved, so
that the administrator and the institution can part company
on intellectual rather than emotional terms.

It must be said that it is very difficult for a dean, personally,
to be the best judge of all these variables. At this juncture, the
dean must rely heavily on his or her staff of associate and assistant deans. These individuals, sitting off to one side of the
line chain of command, are in a better position to sense the
overall mood of the faculty. Because they do not hold the line
power of the dean, they are better receptors of information:
They hear more, they see more. They are told things that
faculty members would not report directly to the dean. To
mix metaphors, they become the radar for the grapevine.
Their candor in sharing these findings with the dean is absolutely essential to the dean's proper assessment of his or her
political power base at any given moment.

Of course, this radar role is not easy to play. The staff assistants to the dean obviously have a personal interest in the
dean's thought processes regarding possible resignation.
They serve at the dean's pleasure and are customarily re-
placed by others when a new dean takes over. Hence, giving the bad news to the boss always produces something of
a boomerang effect on the messenger: "If the dean goes, so
do I!"

Thus, it is easy for a miscalculation to enter into the assessment of support. One can be certain of only one thing,
namely, that support for the dean is always lower than it was
the year before, notwithstanding all the encouragement and
cooperation the dean may have provided and disregarding
the achievements of the college over which he or she presides. Sooner or later, the chips will disappear. Depending on
the momentum of the entire university, the vice-president
must begin pondering the necessity of new leadership.

*In extremis*, the vice-presidency is the dean's primary constituency. It does not take away from or contradict that ob-
servation to assert simultaneously that in the long-term epicycle of governance the dean's decisive constituency is the

142

faculty. So long as that constituency is supportive and cooperative, helping the dean to succeed at the job, the task of leadership expands and matures. In such circumstances a dean may move on to still higher office as a vice-president or president. But, as noted above, when the faculty constituency has received its quota of nos or, in more ugly circumstances, when it energizes the antiadministrator syndrome into a program of sabotage and overt noncooperation designed to make the administrator fail, the dean's effectiveness is at an end.

From a purely institutional point of view, deans, like baseball managers, are expendable. An easy mobility at this level of management provides the institution with periodic occasions for self-examination and renewal, a kind of "seven-year switch." For the dean who does not aspire to a university presidency, the deanship is a fitting episode of service to his or her profession, a temporary suspension of teaching and research for the thankless but also intriguing work of management. When the dean's tour of duty is over, the return to professoring is both a relief and a promotion. The heavy responsibilities are lifted, and the individual is rewarded with the sweet resumption of the life of the tenured full professor—academe's answer to Plato's philosopher-king. It is time for a new dean with a fresh pile of chips.

# NINE

# Evaluating a Dean

GIVEN THE ARRAY of duties and responsibilities of a dean, how do we decide who handles them well and who handles them poorly? Someone has said that America is a nation of scorekeepers. We love statistics, we hunger after lists of the top ten, we hang on the academy awards. In every field, we want to know who are the winners and who are the losers. A stranger stepping into almost any campus in the United States would be able to tell that academic people are well tuned to this scorekeeping syndrome. They have lost interest in grading students but have developed instead an obsession with evaluating each other. If one studies the matrix of steps that go into promotion, tenure, and salary decisions, it is easy to see that evaluation mania is in a very advanced stage in the academy.

Yes, we have developed academic scorekeeping to a high, disciplined art, at least as far as it applies to professors engaged in teaching, research, and service. But what about the administrators, the upper-, middle-, or lower-managers in the enterprise? Is there a coordinate set of standards for them? And, if so, how do we tabulate and rank-order such criteria? More important, what would count as evidence of the presence or absence of each of them in an administrator's conduct?

The evaluation of administrators in other sectors of the American socioeconomy is straightforward, because it is linked closely to the organization's purpose. Businessmen must show a profit. Army generals must keep their forces in fighting readiness and, when war comes, win battles. Bishops must protect the dogma, punish the wayward, and keep the coffers full. Any executive who cannot deliver is fired, demoted, moved laterally to a less sensitive post, or "kicked upstairs" to a harmless staff job.

But what is the link between the academic administrator's work and the purpose of the university? University administration, like other kinds, is essentially personnel management, but the service to be delivered by the personnel— something called higher education—is a fugitive element that defies easy measurement. Accordingly, there is no quick criterion for success or failure in governing the enterprise. As with so much else in university life, we must go in special search of it.

Administrator evaluation is a relatively new phenomenon in higher education. Where it has been tried on an experimental basis, it has turned out to be as time- and money-consuming as the relentless evaluation of professors, if not more so. The beginning stages of this new development, therefore, pose the immediate question of its ultimate cost-effectiveness. Ostensibly, the motivation for managerial measurement is to improve administration throughout the organization. In time, however, each institution will have to determine whether the increments of managerial effectiveness achievable through this device are clearly discernible and, if so, whether the magnitude of those increments justifies the heavy outlay of time and energy of relatively high-priced professionals.

At the outset, administrator evaluation runs into problems of basic strategy not customarily encountered in professor reviews. A central concern is this: when viewing an administrator, does one focus on style or on results? That is, does evaluation mean measuring the dean's personal manner of going about the daily tasks of leadership? Or does evaluation mean determining the quality of the institution that the dean's activities have brought forth?

Other problems arise. Who are to be the judges? In professor evaluation, it is an article of faith that only other—tenured—professors may participate. Does this suggest that deans are to be judged only by other deans or, perhaps, by those slightly higher in the table of organization? And what about a dean's immediate superiors? As colleague administrators, do they join the tribunal, or do they stand to one side to await the results? It is an interesting list of questions, and they all add up to the fact that a dean's work is, indeed, sharply different from that of a professor. The managerial frame of performance and, therefore, of assessment must be constructed on its own, with only indirect linkages to that of a professor.

Taking the questions in reverse order, we begin with jury selection and note at once that the rules differ sharply from those governing a professor review. In a dean review, the judging panel—those hearing the testimony and evaluating the evidence—must always be drawn from personnel outside the dean's own college. It is obvious that the subordinate-superior relationship is much too fragile to permit an exception to this rule.

But when we move beyond the dean's college, still other deviations from faculty practice seem to be called for. As noted, in a professor evaluation, only other professors, senior in rank, are entitled to serve—no administrators, no staff personnel, no junior faculty, no students, no secretaries. When we arrive at administrator evaluation, however, all these groups are consumers of the dean's services. Do they not then belong on the jury? The answer, in the name of judgmental balance, would seem to be yes.

This expansion of the jury to embrace more cosmopolitan interests raises a more far-reaching question of evaluation

146

strategy: should subordinates—faculty and others—sit in judgment of their superiors? In the business community, in the military, and in government agencies, such a suggestion would be ridiculed at the outset—e.g., a lieutenant would not be called upon to evaluate a colonel. Why then should this be permitted in a university?

Understandably, there may be strong differences of opinion on this issue of who may judge a dean. In most universities, a grassroots populism is well entrenched and part of the political environment. Criticism of administrators as a class is common practice. Hence, the evaluation of superiors only formalizes what most faculties would consider their routine, institutional duty. It is a question, however, of whether institutionalizing this criticism and placing it at the center of the evaluation process does not do serious injury to the principle of objectivity and eventually to the integrity of the institution and its administrative groups.

For one thing, a person working in an organization knows very little of the demands of the job at the next rung up. Thus, just as a faculty member is chary of being evaluated by students, owing to their lack of maturity to fully appreciate the professoring art, so likewise is the administrator chary of faculty-level estimates of his or her effectiveness, since professors are relatively unacquainted with the intellectual and emotional pressures under which an administrator must work. For their part, most deans would consider themselves unqualified to evaluate a vice-president or president.

It so happens that faculty members themselves have acknowledged this distinction in their own promotion and tenure procedures. They have adopted a special, well-guarded protocol: to be eligible to sit in judgment of a colleague, one must hold a rank higher than that of the colleague. Of course, some faculty members consider deans to be not of higher rank, but only performing a different, coordinative kind of job. In actual fact, however, deans *are* of higher rank; that's how they came to be chosen as deans. No faculty member really believes that assuming a deanship is merely a lateral move. Hence, if the protocol applies at the professorial level, it necessarily applies at the administrative level. It is imperative that faculty and staff testimony be fully heard concerning a dean's performance, but the evaluation of this testimony should be the work of those directly familiar with managerial responsibilities at the middle and upper levels.

Where does a dean's direct superior fit into all of this? The academic vice-president is the person to whom the dean reports. Does this relationship imply that this individual should serve on the jury, perhaps as its foreman, and play a decisive role? Absolutely not. The vice-president—dean linkage is a special kind of connection. It lives by its own form of colleagueship and mutual trust. Indeed, this very relationship is itself part of what is being evaluated. Hence, it cannot be studied from the inside; it must be studied only by outside, superior observers. This means that neither a dean's direct superior nor that person's staff aides should serve on the evaluation tribunal; neither should these persons be invited to submit testimony. They evaluate the dean's performance every working day. Instead of service on the jury panel, their job is to receive the report and allow its findings to illuminate their own, institutional evaluation of a dean's work.

\* \* \*

Once a jury has been selected, its first job is to determine the criteria by which the dean is to be evaluated. The style-or-results problem cited above is probably specious.[1] Both style and results are vital dimensions of a dean's job, and both must be given great weight. It is obvious that if one focuses on the style or personal attributes of the dean, it would be

[1] In one midwestern university, this puzzle was left to the faculty. A questionnaire was distributed in which all members of the faculty were asked to indicate, by a rank-order type of voting, those elements most relevant to evaluating the dean's performance. The questionnaire appears in appendix C. An alternative to this arrangement, fairer to the administrator and more valuable to the organization, would be to allow the administrators as a group to set the criteria for their own assessment just as professors do. In this manner, those most experienced in managerial work would be involved in determining those elements of performance most central to the job of deaning.

necessary to draw attention to such things as accessibility, warmth, openness, emotional control, fairness, listening ability, decisiveness, firmness under pressure, and the numberless other characterological traits faculty members expect in their executive.[2] In those contacts initiated by the faculty, deans should get high marks for having an open door, for listening to a faculty member's concerns, for welcoming questions and criticism, for being the kind of person one can feel relaxed with, and for being a colleague one can easily talk and readily differ with. These are the qualities for an effective middle manager. Accordingly, deans should get low marks for shutting out the faculty, for contriving an imperial, haughty distance from colleagues, for being defensive when questioned, for losing their composure, and for wobbling and waffling on tough questions in trying to please everybody. These are the signs of weak and ineffective middle management.

Administrative style, however, runs well beyond purely personal traits and embraces a much larger arc of organizational relationship, especially those which a dean initiates and therefore controls. Consultancy is one of these. In the daily work of the organization, the dean consults with others as to the needs of the faculty and the directions of the organization. The information that is shared and the judgments that are passed between the dean and a faculty member are ostensibly the sum total of the transaction. However, the consulting act itself represents a form of nonverbal com-

---

[2] It may be noted in passing that professors themselves do not wish to be evaluated on these characteristics in their own work. Getting into such affective, personality-related areas is expressly forbidden when considering a faculty member for promotion. Only that person's teaching, research, and service—in *objective, documented terms*—are allowable in the dossier. As long-standing as this tradition is, one may question the wisdom of such an antiseptic policy. In some future day, when the affective domain achieves its deserved prominence in American higher education, it might be well for faculties to rethink their habitual exclusion of this side of their makeup. Like administrators, they relate to their colleagues and their students not just as intellectuals but as persons. Their fairness, thoughtfulness, tact, willingness to listen, flexibility, and resilience to the ideas of others are necessary components of their professional, professorial personae.

149

munication with great psychological impact. To seek out an individual for advice is to stroke the ego of that individual. And it is a truism that people who feel good about themselves find it easier to feel good about the organization they work for. An individual is always more disposed to abide by a decision, even if he or she doesn't agree with it, when that decision has been informed by the individual's views on the matter. Characteristically, therefore, the act of consulting itself is an organization-building act. Some deans don't understand this and should be marked down accordingly. They are stingy in sharing the problems of the college with their colleagues, and they work themselves into a position of believing that a decision can be endowed with wisdom from only one head—their own. Other deans have done their psychological homework. Moreover, they know that several insights are better than one or only a few. They therefore consult widely and frequently with those around them, knowing that decisions get carried out more amiably and effectively if their associates share in them. These deans should get high scores.[3]

The rhythm of consultancy may reveal more about a deanship than any other single variable. If it is straightforward and honest, it can be the ongoing medium out of which clear, thoughtful, unambiguous decisions come. But, more important, its daily practice can generate a genuine sense of involvement and participation among the members of the organization, a criterion high on any faculty list of measures by which a dean and the entire organization are to be measured.

[3] It is obvious that a dean may respect some professors' advice more than that of others and therefore have to orchestrate his or her advice-gathering toward the most productive segments of the faculty. Some deans have carried consultancy to a high art, spending most of their time in personal conference or on the telephone seeking out even those views which they know in advance they cannot agree with. If this tendency is carried too far, the faculty may begin to grumble, plead lack of time to spend on college problems, and adopt the view that the administrators should decide those things. In response to such criticism, still other deans keep faculty participation in decisionmaking to a minimum with the understanding that administrative decisions may be challenged if found unacceptable.

Beyond the mode of consultancy lies another closely related medium of style, namely, the dean's own perception of the job, the role he or she wishes to project. Some deans view themselves as ultimate, solitary decisionmakers: those executives who, whether they consult widely or not, gather together facts and ideas and then announce, "We're going to do it this way." Other deans, in contrast, cast themselves in the role of broker and arbitrator, seeing their office as the negotiating center for hammering out consensus in the daily operations of the institution.

Both of these modes of leadership are legitimate and both can lead to strong institutions of high quality. The former, lonely-executive model is effective where wide consultation is the general practice and where problems are studied thoroughly before action is taken. Where there is little consultation, a dean may encounter trouble ahead, since this model levies demands on the faculty that they are sometimes reluctant to grant, namely, a willingness to yield a large sphere of autonomy to the executive and a readiness to abide by decisions once they are made.

The latter, broker style of deaning requires a special blend of liaison skills and, more important, a faculty made up of individuals of basic goodwill and respect for one another. This latter requirement is particularly important, since, as with the previous lonely-executive style, the broker-dean model makes its own special demands on the faculty, namely, a high threshold of tolerance for the grinding hours of committee work that consensus-building requires and a coordinate willingness to accept responsibility for mistakes when they occur. A busy faculty may be reluctant to make such a commitment.

Unfortunately, the brokerage-house deanship labors under a peculiar difficulty. The very presence of a broker in the front office engenders a countervailing, self-cancelling tendency, namely, the intensification of cliques and factions that require brokerage services. Gail Parker, in her brief presidency of Bennington College, found an unsettling example of this.

After three years at Bennington I had come to see that the debate was always the same, and that the better I became at anticipating arguments and negotiating political solutions, the more I strengthened the forces that were pulling the college apart. With a broker ·for president, it was in the interest of faculty members to become lobbyists for particular goods at the expense of the good of the whole.[4]

The brokerage-house deanship may be difficult to sustain indefinitely. If a dean can keep consensus thinking alive, if compromises and mutual assistance pacts continue to be worked out, and if communication among faculty is open and clear, the dean should get a high score for the brokering art. On the other hand, if over time the consensus mentality wavers, communication breaks down, and professors polarize into factional camps, the faculty may need a lonely-executive dean.

The point is that deaning in either mode can be effective. But it is true by definition that a dean cannot simultaneously be both a lonely executive and a consensus-oriented broker; the dean is by choice either one or the other. Hence, the central question for a dean's evaluators is whether the dean's perception of his or her own role is clear and whether performance measures up to that perception.

\* \* \*

Style is a criterion to which each individual may bring a subjective interest and interpretation. The other side of the criterion coin, the quality of results, offers a more objective ground for judgment. If a professor's product is teaching, research, and service, a dean's product is a college, a collectivity of highly educated persons in the business of researching new knowledge and conducting programs for students. Judgments of a college's quality can come from a number of different sources: the national reputation of the faculty, the caliber of teaching they are known by, the amount of exter-

[4]"While Alma Mater Burns," *Atlantic Monthly* 238 (September 1976):41.

nal funding they generate, what the accrediting agencies say, the overall estimate of outsiders from comparable or better institutions, the employability of its graduates, the testimony of those who benefit from its community services or who employ its alumni. In gathering data of this sort, it is important to remember that external judgments of a faculty or the programs they offer must be restricted to those in a position to know. Hence, one caveat is unequivocal: outside referees must be identified by name if their views are to be included. Hearsay, rumor, and gossip are rife in academic circles. In their promotion and tenure reviews, professors are dogged in insisting that anonymous materials be kept out of their files. This hard and fast exclusion applies with equal force to the evaluation of deans.

\* \* \*

Style and results are general rubrics. Inside this global combination lie other, more technical descriptors of managerial work. These are the day-by-day behaviors through which style is exhibited and from which results are produced. Since they serve to fill out the macrocosm of deaning, they bear looking into.

There is in all administration both a logistical, managerial component on the one hand, and a judgmental, leadership component on the other. As for the logistical side, philosopher John Dewey once remarked that administration is essentially keeping people in touch with one another. Management activities are known by different labels; but taken together they represent merely a variation on this keep-in-touch function. This is the subterrain, the underground seam, that defines and gives body to what occurs day by day. Thus, deaning is partly a communications industry; a dean, like other managers, is quintessentially an *information mover*. And by *information* here is meant not merely facts and data, but viewpoints, opinions, hunches, forecasts, predictions of a decision's consequences, and surmises as to the motivations of others.

The other side of administration, the judgmental component, consists in determining what all the information
means, what action it calls for, what responsive attitude it exacts. Deaning, in its leadership phase, is therefore a decisionmaking industry, where the information that is moved about
gets clothed with interest and value. A dean, with the help of
others, attaches significance to bits of information and out of
this generates still more information through his or her executive acts. Priorities of an institution are announced with
each executive decision, not with high-sounding memoranda
of purpose. One by one these decisions accumulate and define the college and give voice to what it wants and where it is
headed.

To consider these two components separately, it is altogether possible that the purely operational side of managerial work could be quantified into measurable units.
Theoretically at least, it might be feasible to determine how
thoroughly a dean moves information around and, more important, whether it gets to the right parties at the right time.
However, deaning is not a mass-media enterprise. Rather,
the communications art is the orchestration of information,
its dissemination in the correct amounts, and its dispatch in
the most effective directions.[5]

Measuring a dean's skills in information movement is obviously difficult. But measuring a dean's wisdom in making
judgments and taking actions—the leadership component—
is even more complex. The fundamental criterion for such
measurement is the effectiveness of the result of the decisions made, the quality of the consequences flowing from the
dean's executive acts. It is obviously true that any given deci-

[5] For example, it is not good management to tell everybody everything. Not only
would information begin to lose its impact, but some actually would not get through.
Being essentially word factories, universities are chronically guilty of information
overload. They operate by a kind of Parkinson's Law of the photocopying machine:
whatever can be copied will be copied, and no matter how many copies are re-
produced, all of them will be distributed. In this shower of paper, beleaguered ad-
dressees lose interest in their mailboxes. The very quantity of information cheapens
its importance in the work of the organization.

sion may later tangle with fortuitous, unforeseen events, or it may set in motion consequences that go far beyond the forecasts of those who are consulted about it. Nevertheless, the only true measure of decisionmaking "in the large" must be a piecemeal analysis of decisionmaking "in the small," that is, the tracing of organizational effects that each decision ultimately yields. The sum total of these yields over the years must stand as the primary criterion for a dean's competence.

\* \* \*

The report prepared as a result of the investigation will come to rest on the desk of the academic vice-president. This individual is customarily responsible not only for academic affairs as such but also for the quality of administrative services performed in all lower echelons. Hence, if the evaluation report is to provoke some institutional response, the vice-president will be the author of such response.

To the jury panel's insights, the vice-president will add his or her own perceptions independently arrived at. From a vice-president's perspective, a rough, general-purpose standard for the performance of lower administrators is how well they keep troubles off his or her desk, how well they keep the waves down. Of course, the ability to keep problems from bouncing to higher levels is a direct function of the authority provided the administrator in question. If this authority is imprecise or unclear, or if end-runs are permitted around it with impunity, then the "bouncing up" of a dean's problems will become chronic, start to snowball, and eventually become unmanageable. In this circumstance, a vice-president or president—or their staff aides—can contribute directly to a dean's ineffectiveness, sometimes without being aware of it.

If, on the other hand, authority lines are clear and consistently held to, and if the vice-president and staff routinely turn back to the dean those complaints that belong in a dean's office, then a vice-president can justifiably count as one performance criterion the degree to which the dean gets

155

problems solved at the college level and does not allow them to float upward to crowd the already prolix agenda at the vice-presidential level.

Before the vice-president prepares a summary response, the evaluated dean should have an opportunity to file his or her own commentary and rebuttal, reflecting on the procedures and conclusions of the jury panel. Following study of the dean's statement, the vice-president would then prepare a formal analysis from the perspective of his or her office. This document should ideally be addressed to the dean, who would then review its contents in a joint conference with the vice-president, the vice-presidential staff, and perhaps the chairperson of the evaluation panel. With this concluding session, the evaluation would be declared over.

\* \* \*

The fall-out of the evaluation—on the dean, faculty, staff, students, fellow deans, and university officers—should be of continuing interest to the institutional hierarchy. All of these groups have a stake in constructive criticism of the administrative services going on around them. This means that the evaluation of a dean must navigate around a natural, built-in hazard, namely, the faculty's predisposition to turn it into a forum for unloading all the gripes, frustrations, and disgruntlements that have accumulated over time. Understandably, the evaluation of a dean would not be scheduled until after several years of service had been completed, meaning that the faculty would have had to absorb the effects of hundreds of administrative decisions. To a faculty in this circumstance, at the tether end of the "no" epoch, the evaluation procedure represents a made-to-order institutionalization of the final skirmish of the adversary relationship, a condition not conducive to objective appraisal.

A mature faculty would not yield to this temptation. In the right hands, with the right spirit brought to it, evaluation can be a very constructive, institution-building exercise. It can illuminate a corner of higher education too long unstudied, namely, the nature of managerial work itself in a university setting. Like everyone else in the academic community, a dean wants to succeed, to learn from mistakes, to enlarge his or her perceptions of leadership, and to grow on the job. Administrative work presents its own peculiar challenges and satisfactions. The invigorating experience of deaning can be materially enhanced by thoughtful, respectful, objective insights on how to do it better and by a full discussion of what is being done well. In this positive, constructive vein, administrator evaluation can make its own special contribution to the quality of academic life.

\* \* \*

As this study draws to a conclusion and one steps back from the job of deaning to view its total contours in perspective, there is revealed an unexpected return to Ground Zero, a kind of cybernetic, feedback phenomenon, namely, how a dean responds to and is therefore affected by those to whom he or she administers. The symbiosis between leader and led is not merely a one-way transfer of energy, but rather a two-way flow of expectations and obligations. Especially in universities, perhaps more so than in public life, the power of citizen professors to shape the ethos and tone of group life is very great. By their conduct, faculty members exhibit their commitment to the college, their identification with its integrity, their determination to help solve its problems, and their pride in the achievements of their colleagues.

Although the dean works hard to engender these feelings, they do not spring into being through his or her hand alone. They find expression in the working spirit of the academic citizen—the university professor who makes a personal response day by day to the demands of pursuing an intellectual career in a group setting. These personal responses to a university environment, taken together, set the conditions in which a dean's leadership moves and lives. Sooner or later the dean's decisionmaking and, in fact, his or her total configuration of managerial style and executive presence must accommodate to these boundary conditions.

There is a sense then in which the evaluation of a dean

turns out to be a kind of mirror, a one-way glass panel through which faculty members can catch a glimpse of their own behavior without being seen. Do they like what they see? Do they like to come to work in the morning, and do they feel good about themselves and their associates when they go home at night? If so, then the chances are good that their college and their dean are doing well.

The evaluation of a dean, therefore, is something more than the close inspection of one person's administrative cleverness. By necessity the investigation looks at everything else too. When all the data are in, all the judgments made, and all the interpretations laid out, what we have is a revelation of the faculty's belief in what they are doing and their belief in each other and in themselves as common partners in an academic adventure. In the end a dean's evaluation turns out to be a faculty's self-portrait.

159

# SIDE 1   INSTRUCTOR AND COURSE EVALUATION SYSTEM

SPECIAL CODE   **For:**

| A | B | C | D | E |
|---|---|---|---|---|
| ⓪ | ⓪ | ⓪ | ⓪ | ⓪ |
| ① | ① | ① | ① | ① |
| ② | ② | ② | ② | ② |
| ③ | ③ | ③ | ③ | ③ |
| ④ | ④ | ④ | ④ | ④ |
| ⑤ | ⑤ | ⑤ | ⑤ | ⑤ |
| ⑥ | ⑥ | ⑥ | ⑥ | ⑥ |
| ⑦ | ⑦ | ⑦ | ⑦ | ⑦ |
| ⑧ | ⑧ | ⑧ | ⑧ | ⑧ |
| ⑨ | ⑨ | ⑨ | ⑨ | ⑨ |

See Side 2 for directions. Use pencil only on this side.

1. When registering, what was your opinion about the

Instructor ○○○
Course ○○○
(Positive / No opinion / Negative)

2. Course in
○ Major
○ Minor
○ Other

3. Sex
○ Male
○ Female

4. This course was
○ Specifically required
○ Required but a choice among several
○ An elective

5. Class
○ Fresh
○ Soph
○ Junior
○ Senior
○ Grad
○ Other

6. Expected Grade
Ⓐ
Ⓑ
Ⓒ
Ⓓ
Ⓔ

|  |  | |  |
|---|---|---|---|
| 1. RATE THE COURSE CONTENT | EXCELLENT | ○○○○○○ | VERY POOR |
| 2. RATE THE INSTRUCTOR | EXCELLENT | ○○○○○○ | VERY POOR |
| 3. RATE THE COURSE IN GENERAL | EXCELLENT | ○○○○○○ | VERY POOR |
| 4. THE COURSE OBJECTIVES WERE: | VERY CLEAR | ①②⑥⑥⑩ | VERY UNCLEAR |
| 5. DID THE INSTRUCTOR PRESENT TOPICS IN A LOGICAL SEQUENCE? | YES, ALMOST ALWAYS | ①②⑥⑥⑩ | NO, ALMOST NEVER |
| 6. DID THE INSTRUCTOR FOLLOW A COURSE OUTLINE? | YES, VERY MUCH | ①②⑥⑥⑩ | NO, NOT AT ALL |
| 7. THE COURSE STRUCK A GOOD BALANCE AMONG READING, DISCUSSION AND WRITING. | TO A GREAT EXTENT | ①②⑥⑥⑩ | NOT AT ALL |
| 8. SHOULD MORE/LESS TIME BE PROVIDED TO REVIEW AND SYNTHESIZE COURSE MATERIAL? | MUCH MORE TIME | ①②⑥⑥⑩ | MUCH LESS TIME |
| 9. I NEEDED MORE DIRECTION. | STRONGLY AGREE | ①②⑥⑥⑩ | STRONGLY DISAGREE |
| 10. HOW WOULD YOU RATE INSTRUCTIONAL MATERIALS USED IN THIS COURSE? | EXCELLENT | ①②⑥⑥⑩ | POOR |
| 11. THE AMOUNT OF READING HOMEWORK ASSIGNED BY THE INSTRUCTOR WAS: | EXCESSIVE | ①②⑥⑥⑩ | NOT ENOUGH |
| 12. DID SUPPLEMENTARY TEXT(S) HELP YOU EXPAND YOUR KNOWLEDGE OF THE MATERIAL? | TO A GREAT EXTENT | ①②⑥⑥⑩ | NOT AT ALL |
| 13. WHAT WAS THE TIME AND EFFORT REQUIRED FOR WRITTEN ASSIGNMENTS? | TOO LONG | ①②⑥⑥⑩ | TOO SHORT |
| 14. SHOULD MORE OR LESS HOMEWORK BE ASSIGNED FOR THIS COURSE? | MUCH MORE | ①②⑥⑥⑩ | MUCH LESS |
| 15. CAN YOU NOW IDENTIFY MAIN POINTS AND CENTRAL ISSUES IN THIS FIELD? | YES, CLEARLY | ①②⑥⑥⑩ | NOT VERY WELL |
| 16. DID YOU IMPROVE YOUR ABILITY TO APPLY PRINCIPLES IN NEW SITUATIONS? | YES, SIGNIFICANTLY | ①②⑥⑥⑩ | NO, NOT MUCH |
| 17. DID YOU IMPROVE YOUR ABILITY TO SOLVE REAL PROBLEMS IN THIS FIELD? | YES, SIGNIFICANTLY | ①②⑥⑥⑩ | NO, NOT REALLY |
| 18. DID YOU LEARN MUCH ABOUT CAREER OPPORTUNITIES? | YES, QUITE A LOT | ①②⑥⑥⑩ | NO, NOT MUCH |
| 19. DID THIS COURSE INCREASE YOUR INTEREST IN THE SUBJECT MATTER? | YES, GREATLY | ①②⑥⑥⑩ | NO, NOT MUCH |
| 20. DID THIS COURSE MAINTAIN YOUR ATTENTION THROUGHOUT THE SEMESTER? | ALMOST ALWAYS | ①②⑥⑥⑩ | ALMOST NEVER |
| 21. WERE YOU STIMULATED TO DO EXTRA READING ABOUT THE COURSE MATERIAL? | YES, VERY MUCH | ①②⑥⑥⑩ | NO, NOT REALLY |
| 22. WERE YOU STIMULATED TO DISCUSS RELATED TOPICS WITH FRIENDS OUTSIDE OF CLASS? | YES, OFTEN | ①②⑥⑥⑩ | NO, NEVER |
| 23. COMPARED TO OTHER COURSES, HOW MUCH EFFORT DID YOU PUT INTO THIS COURSE? | MUCH MORE | ①②⑥⑥⑩ | MUCH LESS |
| 24. I WENT TO SLEEP IN CLASS: | VERY OFTEN | ①②⑥⑥⑩ | NEVER |
| 25. I LEARNED MORE FROM THE READINGS THAN I DID FROM LECTURES AND CLASS DISCUSSIONS. | STRONGLY AGREE | ①②⑥⑥⑩ | STRONGLY DISAGREE |
| 26. WAS THE INSTRUCTOR A GOOD SPEAKER? | YES, VERY GOOD | ①②⑥⑥⑩ | NO, RATHER POOR |

**DO NOT WRITE**

**IN THE**

**SHADED**

**AREA**

Please use this side of the form for your personal comments on teacher effectiveness and other aspects of the course. Use pencil only in responding to the objective questions on the reverse side.

Objective items 1 - 3 will be used to compare this course and instructor to others in the department and institution. Data from other items after item 3 would be useful to the instructor for course improvements. Your instructor will not see your completed evaluation until final grades are in for your course.

NOTE:

Someone other than your instructor should collect and mail these forms.

**PLEASE WRITE COMMENTS BELOW**

**A**

What are the major strengths and weaknesses of the instructor?

**B**

What aspects of this course were most beneficial to you?

**C**

What do you suggest to improve this course?

**D**

Comment on the grading procedures and exams.

**E**

Instructor option question

**F**

Instructor option question

# INSTRUCTOR AND COURSE EVALUATION FORM 37* — UNIVERSITY OF ILLINOIS AT CHICAGO CIRCLE

INSTRUCTOR'S NAME: _____   COURSE NO. _____

Please use this form to anonymously evaluate the instructor and subject matter of this course. For each question, indicate your view by blackening the appropriate space with a #2 pencil.

## PART I — BACKGROUND INFORMATION

**1. Your current class standing.**

| FR | SOPH | JR | SR | GRAD | OTHER |
|----|------|----|----|------|-------|
| :::: | :::: | :::: | :::: | :::: | :::: |

**2. Your cumulative GPA at the beginning of this quarter.**

| BELOW 2.49 | 2.50-2.99 | 3.00-3.49 | 3.50-3.99 | 4.00-4.49 | 4.50-5.00 | GPA NOT YET ESTABLISHED |
|-----------|-----------|-----------|-----------|-----------|-----------|------------------------|
| :::: | :::: | :::: | :::: | :::: | :::: | :::: |

**3. What grade do you expect to get in this course?**

| A | B | C | D | E | PASS | OTHER |
|---|---|---|---|---|------|-------|
| :::: | :::: | :::: | :::: | :::: | :::: | :::: |

**4. Your reason for taking this course.**

| REQUIRED OR FOUNDATION | ELECTIVE |
|------------------------|----------|
| :::: | :::: |

**5. Type of course.**

| IN MAJOR AREA | NOT IN MAJOR AREA |
|---------------|-------------------|
| :::: | :::: |

**6. How difficult has this course been for you?**

| VERY EASY | EASY | NEITHER EASY NOR DIFFICULT | DIFFICULT | VERY DIFFICULT |
|-----------|------|----------------------------|-----------|----------------|
| :::: | :::: | :::: | :::: | :::: |

## PART II — EVALUATION: EACH OF THE DIMENSIONS BELOW HAS SEVERAL ITEMS THAT ARE TO BE ANSWERED:

YES, if the item describes the dimension
?, if you cannot decide if the item applies, or
NO, if the item does not describe the dimension

### INSTRUCTOR IN CLASS

| | YES | ? | NO | |
|---|-----|---|-----|---|
| 2. | :::: | :::: | :::: | Confusing |
| 4. | :::: | :::: | :::: | Enjoyable |
| 6. | :::: | :::: | :::: | Logical |
| 8. | :::: | :::: | :::: | Thorough |

| | YES | ? | NO | |
|---|-----|---|-----|---|
| 1. | :::: | :::: | :::: | Stimulating |
| 3. | :::: | :::: | :::: | Clear |
| 5. | :::: | :::: | :::: | Constructive |
| 7. | :::: | :::: | :::: | Exciting |
| 9. | :::: | :::: | :::: | Thought provoking |

### TEXT AND/OR OTHER REQUIRED READINGS   If there were no text or other readings, blacken this

space :::: and go on to the next section.

| | YES | ? | NO | |
|---|-----|---|-----|---|
| 11. | :::: | :::: | :::: | Good |
| 13. | :::: | :::: | :::: | Worthwhile |
| 15. | :::: | :::: | :::: | Interesting |

| | YES | ? | NO | |
|---|-----|---|-----|---|
| 10. | :::: | :::: | :::: | Enjoyable |
| 12. | :::: | :::: | :::: | Useless |
| 14. | :::: | :::: | :::: | Practical |
| 16. | :::: | :::: | :::: | Important |

SUBJECT MATTER

| | YES | ? | NO | |
|---|---|---|---|---|
| 19. | ::::: | ::::: | ::::: | Challenging |
| 21. | ::::: | ::::: | ::::: | Relevant |
| 23. | ::::: | ::::: | ::::: | Valuable |
| 25. | ::::: | ::::: | ::::: | Practical |
| 27. | ::::: | ::::: | ::::: | Enjoyable |

| | YES | ? | NO | |
|---|---|---|---|---|
| 20. | ::::: | ::::: | ::::: | Interesting |
| 22. | ::::: | ::::: | ::::: | Bad |
| 24. | ::::: | ::::: | ::::: | Significant |
| 26. | ::::: | ::::: | ::::: | Stimulating |

GRADED ASSIGNMENTS AND EXAMINATIONS  If there were no graded assignments or examinations, blacken this space ::::: and go on to next section.

| | YES | ? | NO | |
|---|---|---|---|---|
| 28. | ::::: | ::::: | ::::: | Valuable |
| 30. | ::::: | ::::: | ::::: | Fair |
| 32. | ::::: | ::::: | ::::: | Tricky |
| 34. | ::::: | ::::: | ::::: | Vague |
| 36. | ::::: | ::::: | ::::: | Bad |

| | YES | ? | NO | |
|---|---|---|---|---|
| 29. | ::::: | ::::: | ::::: | Ambiguous |
| 31. | ::::: | ::::: | ::::: | Clearly defined |
| 33. | ::::: | ::::: | ::::: | Distasteful |
| 35. | ::::: | ::::: | ::::: | Clear |

SPECIAL QUESTIONS  If instructor provided additional questions, use this section for responding. Otherwise, blacken this space ::::: and go on to the next section.

| | YES | ? | NO |
|---|---|---|---|
| 37. | ::::: | ::::: | ::::: |
| 39. | ::::: | ::::: | ::::: |
| 41. | ::::: | ::::: | ::::: |
| 43. | ::::: | ::::: | ::::: |

| | YES | ? | NO |
|---|---|---|---|
| 38. | ::::: | ::::: | ::::: |
| 40. | ::::: | ::::: | ::::: |
| 42. | ::::: | ::::: | ::::: |

GENERAL EVALUATION QUESTIONS  All things considered, how would you rate each of the following compared with all other courses and instructors you've had?

| | BOTTOM 10% | NEXT 20% | MID 40% | NEXT 20% | TOP 10% |
|---|---|---|---|---|---|
| 44. Instructor | ::::: | ::::: | ::::: | ::::: | ::::: |
| 45. Subject Matter | ::::: | ::::: | ::::: | ::::: | ::::: |
| 46. Text and/or other required readings. | ::::: | ::::: | ::::: | ::::: | ::::: |

PART III — GENERAL COMMENTS  Please comment on what you liked most and/or least about this course and what the instructor might do to improve it. Please use the reverse side of this form for comments.

* adapted from Course Evaluation Instrument, copyright 1974 by University of Wisconsin System. Used by permission.

1. *Teaching ability, curriculum development, and performance.*

After a summary introduction, the assessment should address itself to the following questions when applicable:

A. List the courses the candidate has taught each quarter for the
past three years. What is the relevance of these courses to the department's curriculum?

B. What measures has the department used to evaluate teaching
effectiveness? Summarize results of these evaluations, but do not
forward unanalyzed raw data derived from formal teaching evaluations. Summarized results should be compared to department
and/or college and/or university norms. Type of student evaluation
used should be specified.

C. What is the assessment of the nominee's impact on the quality
of student performance?

D. Give the names of graduate students supervised, the thesis
titles, and beginning and completion dates for the degree work.

E. To what extent has the nominee attempted to improve the
quality of teaching? Have these efforts been successful?

F. Has the nominee made contributions to curriculum development (development of new teaching methods or materials) beyond

what is expected of all teachers in meeting classroom obligations? How have these contributions been evaluated?

G. How has the nominee's teaching ability been recognized on campus?

H. If the nominee has presented lectures or seminars at another university while on the UICC faculty, the evaluation of members of the profession outside the department whose judgment has bearing on the proposed promotion is appropriate. If letters from senior colleagues evaluating instructional effectiveness are applicable, they should be attached.

I. Testimonials from individual students are discouraged.

### 2. *Research, creative, and other scholarly activities.*

After a summary introduction, the assessment should address itself to the following when applicable:

A. Post graduate awards, fellowships, lectureships, professional consulting, and other evidence of merit or recognition related to the nominee's professional development, with dates and brief explanation of the nature of the award.

B. Grant support. Please use the attached form (on p. 166) for this purpose.

   (1) External sources.
   (2) University sources.

C. Research, creative, and other scholarly works:

   (1) Publications prior to last personnel action.
   (2) List of publications since last personnel action (i.e., promotion or appointment). Refereed journals should be indicated by an asterisk in the left margin. In cases of joint authorship, indicate senior author when relevant by underlining. Give complete bibliographical references.
      a) Published works.
      b) Work actually in the press.
      c) Work accepted for publication.
   (3) Papers presented at professional meetings.
   (4) Other creative or scholarly works, e.g., list of performances, exhibitions, and the like; critical assessments of creative work by outside evaluators (with biographical in-

Name _____  Department _____  Date _____

## SPONSORED RESEARCH ACTIVITIES

Please list all proposals for the last five years regardless whether funded or not. Include both external and internal agencies.

| Date Submitted | Role of Nominee as Specified in Grant* | Title of Proposal | REQUESTED | | APPROVED | |
|---|---|---|---|---|---|---|
| | | | Agency or Board | Amount | Amount Funded | Period From  To |
| | | | | | | |
| | | | | | | |

*Use language of grant application.

formation as in 2D); reviews. Indicate whether or not an exhibition is juried.

(5) Brief summary of work in progress.

D. The head should obtain the written evaluation of at least three members of the profession outside the campus whose judgment has bearing on a proposed promotion. No more than one may be from a professor who taught the nominee at the university which awarded the nominee's highest degree or from a graduate of that university who was a student contemporary of the nominee. Identify outside evaluators by entering a brief biographical sketch for each of them. Referee reports on the candidate's works, if available, should also be submitted. Letters of evaluation should be attached. Please attach a copy of the letter used to solicit the reviews of outside evaluators. Specify who nominated outside evaluators and any past or present relationship between evaluator and nominee at end of biographical sketch (e.g., former colleague, dissertation director).

E. The research, creative and scholarly goals of the nominee, and the relation the nominee's achievements and promise for future achievements have with respect to these goals.

*3. Service: General usefulness to the university,
including professional activities and university-related external activities
utilizing professional expertise.*

After a summary introduction indicating areas of outstanding service, the assessment should address itself to the following when applicable:

A. Administrative responsibility, at present or at any time since last promotion, with inclusive dates.

B. Special contributions to the development of the academic unit's overall educational program (e.g., designing and implementing field work curricula, furtherance of academic mission, departmental committee work); special contributions beyond the unit.

C. Service within the university: significant committee assignments held since last promotion, with inclusive dates. When applicable, the head should obtain written statements from committee chairpersons outside the department assessing the nature and effectiveness of the nominee's committee work. These should be attached. Indicate whether the nominee was appointed or elected.

(1) College committees

(2) University committees

D. Nonuniversity professional activities, such as offices held in professional organizations, editorships, etc., with inclusive dates.

E. External activities based on professional expertise and related to the university's public service objectives. Indicate whether related to the individual's professional competence or to the unit's mission. Suggested outline:

Project description          Duration

(1) Workshops

(2) Staff development of personnel of external agencies

(3) If external activities are significant part of the nominee's service, the head should obtain the evaluation of external referees whose judgment has bearing on the proposed promotion (the head's evaluation of such activities should be included). These should be attached.

(4) Advancement of the discipline by outside activities.

## CRITERIA FOR EVALUATING A DEAN

### *Criteria for an Administrative Evaluation*

The following items represent criteria that a fact-finder and an evaluator might use as a basis for evaluating an administrator:

1. Leadership of the unit
2. Leadership to related agencies in the external world
3. A talent finder and builder of the unit
4. Planning ability
5. Accessibility and communication with various constituencies
6. Resource allocation
7. Overall effectiveness, i.e., output of the unit

In an attempt to develop areas of concern for the administrative evaluation, this appendix is divided into two parts. The first section outlines criteria that a fact-finder and an evaluator would bring to a particular administrator. The second part lists some types of specific information required to carry out a particular evaluation in the context of the stipulated criteria.

1. Leadership at the institution
   A. Staff relations
      (1) Sensitivity and perceptiveness in working with people
      (2) Recognition of staff and faculty accomplishments

(3) Interest and concern for helping those who require service

(4) Candor, openness, honesty, credibility

B. Leadership

(1) Project a vision that is understandable

(2) Offer fresh ideas or respond to them

(3) Inspire a desire for excellence in faculty and staff

(4) Establish an esprit de corps in the unit

(5) Flexibility in administering

Some specific types of information that might yield data would include:

A. Staff relations

(1) Outside offers vs. retention rate of unit members

(2) Reasons for staff departure

(3) Number and nature of positive remarks about administrator

B. Leadership

(1) Existence of a scope and mission statement for the unit that is well understood and accepted

(2) Innovative programs underway or planned, and support of established values

(3) Demands on administrator for consulting and lecturing purposes

2. Leadership to related agencies in the external world

A. Influential in the formation of external policies affecting the unit, i.e., state or federal educational policies

B. Nature of interaction between administrator and pertinent state and federal agencies

C. Perception by peer group (other administrators)

D. Amount of outside support generated by administrator for the unit

E. Participation in pertinent seminars, workshops, task forces, and similar activities

F. Awareness of those people in similar positions at other institutions

Some specific types of information that might yield data in this area would include:

   A. Number and types of memberships on external committees, commissions, and similar service groups
   B. Experienced interviewer's impressions after discussions
   with members of peer group re influence and respect
3. A talent finder and builder of the unit
   A. Staff selection and promotion
      (1) Quality of personnel filling new positions and key
      posts
      (2) A good judge of talent
      (3) Young staff understand what is expected of them
      (4) Delegation of responsibility in ways that are consistent
      with staff growth
      (5) Ability to continue the professional growth and schol-
      arship of members of the unit
   B. Staff relations
      (1) Effectiveness with students, faculty, staff, and other
      administrators
      (2) People's awareness of issues facing the unit
      (3) Resolution of conflicts
      (4) Encouragement of divergent viewpoints
      (5) Stimulation of the consideration of change or differ-
      ing approaches
      (6) Handling of matters such as granting of tenure, ad-
      vancements, setting workloads, and personnel matters
      (7) Allocation of clerical assistance, travel funds, staff
      equipment funds, space, graduate awards, lecture
      funds, other expense funds
   C. Policies and Programs
      (1) Ability to implement needed programs
      (2) Support and implementation of the policies of the
      unit
      (3) Communication of the needs of the unit to superiors
      (4) Development of standards of quality for members of
      the unit
      (5) Implementation of personnel and program evalua-
      tions of the unit

Some specific types of information that might yield data in
these areas would include:

A. Staff selection and promotion
   (1) Salary and promotional data—average time between promotions by rank and sex
   (2) External recognition of staff members (e.g., *Who's Who*, advisory appointments, prizes and awards)
   (3) Faculty turnover data and evaluations of departed members who were considered to be of high potential
   (4) Dollar amount of research and contract grants awarded to members of the unit
   (5) Number of copyrights and patents awarded to members of the unit
   (6) Number of published (or unpublished) writings of staff related to advancement of amount and quality of knowledge in field
   (7) Judged quality of above writings
B. Staff relations
   (1) Faculty activity data showing faculty FTE effort and associated salary cost for each of several categories of activities
   (2) Ratio of FTE staff per FTE student
   (3) Appropriateness of workload to each staff member
C. Policies and Programs
   (1) Quality of programs as viewed by outside authorities (e.g., ACE ratings)
   (2) Criteria for personnel evaluation established and written down at the time of hiring of new members
   (3) Student evaluations of courses and instructors
   (4) Proportion of staff involvement on program improvement

4. Planning ability
A. Direction and goals
   (1) Identifiable set of goals which are educationally significant (of high quality)
   (2) Existence of an identifiable set of goals which are realistic in terms of the capacities of the unit (budgetary staff)
B. Staff relations
   (1) Ascertainment of the needs of the unit
   (2) Identification of key people to help map future

(3) Stimulation of members to work effectively and cooperatively toward these goals

(4) Balance of staff consultation with timely decisiveness in decisionmaking

C. Organization

(1) Understanding of which organizational tasks will benefit from detailed planning and which will not

(2) Timing, i.e., knowing when planning is warranted

(3) Completion of stated tasks

(4) Organization of personal office operations

D. Evaluation of plans

(1) Establishment of program evaluation procedures and study of the criteria

(2) Study of staff characteristics—distribution by age, rank, salary, sex, ethnic

(3) Study of research activities done by unit

Some specific types of information that might yield data would include:

A. Direction and goals

(1) Development of scope and mission statement and judgment of its integration of purpose with the larger unit

B. Staff relations

(1) Staff's sense of accomplishment

(2) General feeling that chief administrator has control of situations and is providing a direction

(3) Staff feeling that they are involved in important and meaningful projects

(4) Staff's sense of commitment to the unit, i.e., are they optimistic and excited about the future?

C. Organization

(1) Delineation of functions and job descriptions for staff members

(2) Existence of accepted and used administrative guidelines

5. Accessibility and communication

A. Personnel relations

(1) Intellectual accessibility, i.e., ability to listen and be influenced by cogent arguments

        (2) Procedural accessibility, i.e., can members of the unit and significant others tell how important decisions are made, where they are made, and why?
- B. Effectiveness of communication
  - (1) Dissemination of information, i.e., are members of the unit informed about decisions, impending decisions, and new developments on issues?
  - (2) Response to requests for information and direction
  - (3) Interpretation of policy to other people
  - (4) Existence of an atmosphere for open communication among all segments of the unit

Most of this information is attitudinal in nature and probably should be collected through an interview. Some interview questions might consist of the following:
- A. Personnel relations
  - (1) Do people feel they can get individual appointments when they think it necessary without excessively long waits?
  - (2) Do people feel that all sides of a major issue have been thoroughly considered before a decision is made?
- B. Effectiveness of communication
  - (1) Do people feel well informed about the issues and controversies and feel they have had an opportunity to express a view if they desire?
  - (2) Do people feel they know about the major issues confronting the unit?
  - (3) Are letters generally responded to quickly?
  - (4) Is there a unit newsletter? If so, what kind of information does it contain?

6. Resource allocation
   - A. Budget preparation
     - (1) Approach to budgetmaking process considering the total needs of the unit
     - (2) Effectiveness of bargaining with superiors during the budgetary bargaining period
   - B. Distribution of resources
     - (1) Process to phase out unnecessary or wasteful programs

      (2) Process for reallocation of resources in times of scarcity

      (3) Sharing of resources

      (4) Realization of the dollar cost of own proposals

C. Control of resources

      (1) Discrimination between instances when dollars are well spent and poorly spent

      (2) Control of expenditures

Some specific types of information that might yield data would include:

A. Budget preparation

      (1) Study of priorities and their relation to budget requests

      (2) Study of capital and operating-budget requests and comparison with yearly allocation

B. Distribution of resources

      (1) Faculty activity data—FTE effort and associated salary cost for each of several categories of activities

      (2) Amount of funds and kinds of projects supported by outside funds

      (3) Staff salary data, racial-ethnic data

      (4) Proportion of budget allocated to program development or improvement

C. Control of resources

      (1) Differences between expenditures and income for a specified period of time

      (2) Study of unit costs of activities

7. Total effectiveness, i.e., output of unit

Determining the context of this item would depend upon the contract established by the supervisor and the administrator. The expectations and conditions discussed around the categories of role, style, and technique should ultimately be synthesized during any evaluation process to describe a general success factor for the delivery of administration. Obviously, differing combinations of response to the same criteria could result in equivalent evaluations—as usual, flexibility and good sense are at a premium in this judgment stage.

*Faculty Questionnaire*

Check the ten items in the following you believe should be given the greatest emphasis in evaluating the dean of the college:

1. Leadership of the college
   A. Staff relations
   ———(1) Sensitivity and perceptiveness in working with people
   ———(2) Recognition of staff and faculty accomplishments
   ———(3) Interest and concern for helping those who require service
   ———(4) Candor, openness, honesty, credibility
   B. Leadership
   ———(1) Projection of a vision that is understandable
   ———(2) Source of fresh ideas or response to ideas from others
   ———(3) Inspiration for excellence in faculty and staff
   ———(4) Establishment of esprit de corps in the college
   ———(5) Flexibility in administering

2. Leadership in the external world
   ———A. Influence in formation of local, state, and federal policies affecting college
   ———B. Interaction with local, state, and federal agencies
   ———C. Rating by deans at other colleges of education
   ———D. Generation of outside support
   ———E. Participation in pertinent seminars, workshops, task forces
   ———F. Acquaintance with deans at other institutions

3. Talent finder and builder of unit
   A. Staff selection and promotion
   ———(1) Quality of personnel filling new positions and in key posts
   ———(2) Ability to judge talent
   ———(3) Definition of positions of young staff
   ———(4) Delegation of responsibility as consistent with staff growth
   ———(5) Encouragement of faculty professional growth and scholarship

176

B. Staff relations

———(1) Effectiveness with students, faculty, staff, and other administrators

———(2) Faculty awareness of issues facing unit

———(3) Resolution of conflicts

———(4) Encouragement of divergent viewpoints

———(5) Stimulation of change or new approaches

———(6) Handling of personnel matters such as promotion, tenure, and workloads

———(7) Allocation of resources such as clerical assistance, travel funds, equipment funds, and other expense funds

C. Policies and programs

———(1) Implementation of needed programs

———(2) Implementation of policies of the college

———(3) Communication of college needs to superiors

———(4) Development of standards of quality for the faculty

———(5) Implementation of college personnel and program evaluations

4. Planning ability

A. Direction and goals

———(1) Establishment of educationally significant goals for college

———(2) Establishment of realistic goals for college

B. Staff relations

———(1) Identification of needs of college

———(2) Identification of key people to plan future

———(3) Stimulation of faculty to work as a team toward goals

———(4) Balance of faculty consultation with decisiveness

C. Organization

———(1) Identification of appropriate planning tasks

———(2) Timing of planning

———(3) Completion of planning tasks

———(4) Organization of dean's office

D. Evaluation of plans

———(1) Program evaluation criteria and procedures

————(2) Distribution of faculty and staff by age, rank, salary, sex, and ethnic origin

————(3) Research activity of college

5. Accessibility and communication
   A. Personal relations
   ————(1) Intellectual accessibility—influenced by cogent arguments
   ————(2) Procedural accessibility—do faculty and staff know how, where, and why decisions are made
   B. Effectiveness of communication
   ————(1) Keeping faculty informed
   ————(2) Response to requests for information and direction
   ————(3) Interpretation of policy to others
   ————(4) Existence of open atmosphere in college

6. Resource allocation
   A. Budget preparation
   ————(1) Consideration of total needs of unit
   ————(2) Effectiveness in bargaining with superiors
   B. Distribution of resources
   ————(1) Procedure for phasing out programs
   ————(2) Procedure for allocating scarce resources
   ————(3) Distribution of resources
   ————(4) Consideration of cost of personnel proposals
   C. Control of resources
   ————(1) Discrimination between good and poor expenditures
   ————(2) Control of expenditures

7. Total effectiveness
   ————A. Overall quality of the output of the college

8. If there are any topics not covered in the above list that definitely should be considered in the evaluation of the dean of the college, list them below. These should be topics that you would list in the top ten in importance:

_____
_____
_____
_____
_____

9. Identification data
   A. Rank (check one) ———Professor
                        ———Associate professor
                        ———Assistant professor
                        ———Instructor
                        ———Lecturer
                        ———Visiting appointment
                        ———Adjunct appointment
   B. Tenure status (check one) ———Tenured
                                ———Nontenured
   C. Years on faculty ———

*Topical Interview Guide*

1. Organization of the college.

2. Leadership in the external world.

3. Leadership in the college.

4. Dean's role in planning and establishing goals.

5. Staff relations and developing teamwork.

6. Relations and bargaining with superior administrators.

7. Dean's accessibility and effectiveness in communication.

8. How satisfied are you with your role in the college?

9. Any other comments, including your perception of the dean's weaknesses and strengths.

*Index*

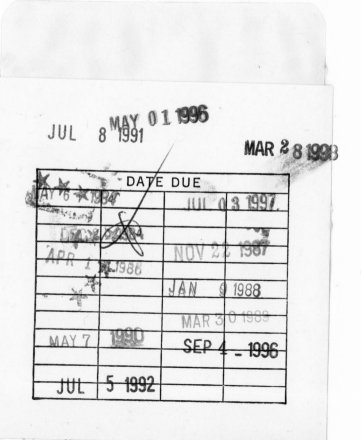